Old Theatres in the Potteries

William A. Neale

Old Theatres in the Potteries

© 2010 William A. Neale. All Rights Reserved.
ISBN 978-1-4466-3846-0

First Edition, October 2010

Typeset in Adobe Garamond LT

All photographs contained within this book were taken by the author with the exception of the postcards of the Grand Theatre, Hanley and Empire Theatre, Longton.

The illustrations of the Theatre Royal, Hanley, Empire Theatre, Hanley and Empire Theatre, Longton are also the work of the author.

A Note from The Author

This book hopes to chronicle the history of the theatres opened in the Potteries through to the opening of the Victoria Theatre, Hartshill in 1962, starting in the north of the area and working south. It also covers several of the notable music halls and concert venues, including the Victoria Hall, along with the permanent circus buildings which were also erected for the people of the Potteries.

For such a small area there were a surprisingly large number of theatres over the years, with every town in the area with the exception of poor old Fenton at some point possessing its own theatre. Perhaps this was due to fearsome competition between the five towns, attempting to outdo one other with larger and even more expensively appointed temples of Thespis. One has to remember that until the federation in 1910, each town (Tunstall, Burslem, Hanley, Stoke, Fenton and Longton) was independent of one another.

Some of the many theatres were successful, some were financial disasters, and some have resulted in prison and bankruptcy for their owners. Quite a few have burst mysteriously into flame, and only a very small number can be seen in the city of Stoke-on-Trent today.

The large theatre programme collection at the *Stoke-on-Trent City Archives*, which I had a hand in cataloguing, has proved of great help in writing this book, providing many of the illustrations within. Their collection of vintage local newspapers, directories and maps has also been of use. The newspaper digitisation projects of *The Times, The Guardian, The Stage* and the British Library have also proved immensely helpful, throwing up information that I doubt that I would have discovered otherwise. One can only imagine what else will be unearthed when the *Staffordshire Advertiser* and *Evening Sentinel* undergo the same treatment.

I have tried to ensure that everything written here is as accurate as possible, however I apologise in the event that errors have slipped in.

William A. Neale, October 2010
The author can be contacted by email
williamneale@bhamalumni.org

With Thanks to

Chris Latimer and the staff of the
Stoke-on-Trent City Archives

Liz Cooper
Martin Hassall
Moira Lewis
Mandy Pover
Barbara Rogerson
Phillip Wheeler

The former staff of the
Horace Barks Reference Library
and the other Stoke-on-Trent Libraries
for seeing a future use for
theatrical ephemera

Laura Naylor and Liz Rowley at *The Sentinel*

Mr. Powell for answering my letter in *All Our Yesterdays*

The Staff of Liquid Nightclub, Hanley for their
information concerning the current condition
of the Theatre Royal building

The Victoria and Albert Museum for allowing me to
include the George Cooke illustration

Contents

Introduction 7

Prince of Wales Theatre, Tunstall 9

Poynter's New Theatre, Burslem 13

Snape's Theatre, Burslem 14

Wedgwood Theatre, Burslem 19

Queen's Theatre, Burslem 23

Coliseum Theatre of Varieties, Burslem 27

Theatre Royal, Hanley 31

Circus Music Hall, Hanley 70

People's Music Hall, Hanley 73

Imperial Circus, Hanley 76

Gaiety Theatre of Varieties, Hanley 81

Batty's Circus, Hanley 82

Victoria Hall, Hanley 85

Empire Theatre, Hanley 91

Lyric Hall, Hanley 95

Grand Theatre of Varieties, Hanley 97

Regent Theatre, Hanley 105

Century Theatre, Hanley 112

Mitchell Memorial Theatre, Hanley 113

Victoria Theatre, Hartshill 115

Crown Theatre, Stoke 123

Gordon Theatre and Opera House, Stoke 125

Repertory Theatre, Stoke 135

Royal Alma Theatre, Longton 137

Royal Victoria Theatre, Longton 139

Queen's Theatre, Longton 143

Panopticon Theatre, Longton 161

Regent Theatre, Longton 163

Introduction

The first permanent theatre in the area, as we would think of one today, was the Theatre Royal in Newcastle-under-Lyme which opened in 1788. Two of the shareholders in this venture were Josiah Spode and Josiah Wedgwood, and it was successful for many decades before closing towards the end of the nineteenth century. It later found a use as one of Newcastle's first cinemas.[1]

Within the six towns however it took much longer to establish such a venue, although several attempts were made in the early years of the nineteenth century. In August 1820 H. H. Williamson, John Wood, John Henry Clive, Joseph Brindley and Thomas Cox met to form a theatre, but nothing came from this attempt. 1824 saw another scheme, with fifty subscribers including Richard Edensor Heathcote of Longton Hall, the Spodes (senior and junior), H. H. Williamson, Jesse Breeze, William Adams and Henry Magnus. This would have created a "Temple of Thespis" with a temporary pit for equestrian performances, however the venture failed before any construction work began[2].

That is not to say that the Staffordshire Potteries were devoid of entertainments in the first half of the nineteenth century. Travelling showmen toured the country and pitched up in the area, acting from the back of their travelling stages. Several were known to be operating in the area including Duval, Seagrave, Thorne, Stephen Pickhull, Matthew Wardhaugh and John Snape. The last two took up residence in the area and set up permanent theatres later in the century.

Entertainment was also found in the public houses. 'The Sea Lion' in Hanley was said to be one of the chief places of entertainment[3], with the large yard behind the inn playing host to plays and circuses. Music was also a prominent feature inside the pubs and inns of the time, eventually spawning the music hall. Before the Church Street circus and Victoria Hall were opened, the old Hanley Market served as a home for large concerts. With the stalls moved away it played host to big names including "Swedish Nightingale" Jenny Lind who performed in April 1868.

It was not until 1852 that the six towns gained a legitimate theatre of their own, the Royal Pottery Theatre in Hanley, which would be the first of many opened in the area over the years.

Old Theatres in the Potteries

Prince of Wales Theatre, Tunstall

The Burslem and Tunstall Prince of Wales Theatre was sited on Booth's Fields at the junction of Sneyd Street and Victoria Street, now Ladywell Street and Harewood Street[4].

This was not the first theatre in Tunstall. On 8th March 1851, Loore and James opened a theatre with a production of 'The Wood Demon', although this was highly likely to be a temporary, wooden structure[5]. In 1864, Arthur Taylor applied for a licence for a wooden theatre in Tunstall[6], which may or may not have opened that year, however a license was subsequently awarded to Taylor for a new brick theatre.

The Prince of Wales Theatre was opened on Monday 2nd October 1865 for the winter season, operated by Arthur Taylor and Mr. T. Roberts. The architects were Wards of Hanley with construction by Mr. Harley of Burslem. The total cost, including building, scenery and wardrobe was said to be £3,000. 1,500 audience members could be seated in the new building over stalls and pit, boxes and gallery[7]. Illumination was provided by gaslight, and the venue was advertised as being the "largest, most complete and best arranged theatre in Staffordshire"[8]. The local press did note however that the floor of the gallery blocked the view from many of the boxes, and that no lobby was provided for these seats.

Opening night saw proprietor Arthur Taylor address the gathered audience in rhyme, promising them that the theatre would be conducted with every regard to "decency and morality". The opening week consisted mainly of double-bills of Shakespeare paired with farces.

Unfortunately Taylor and Roberts were bankrupt just two years later[9].

The building presented some of the top touring stars of the day, including tragedian Gustavus V. Brooke. Operas were also presented, including 'Faust' and 'Don Giovanni' and pantomimes such as 'King Pippin'.

Above Image. The former Prince of Wales Theatre, Tunstall, on the corner of Ladywell Road and Harewood Street. July 2010.

Having stood as a Salvation Army Barracks for over a century, the building is now home to a local ceramics company.

Below Image. Same as above. Side Elevation.

Old Theatres in the Potteries

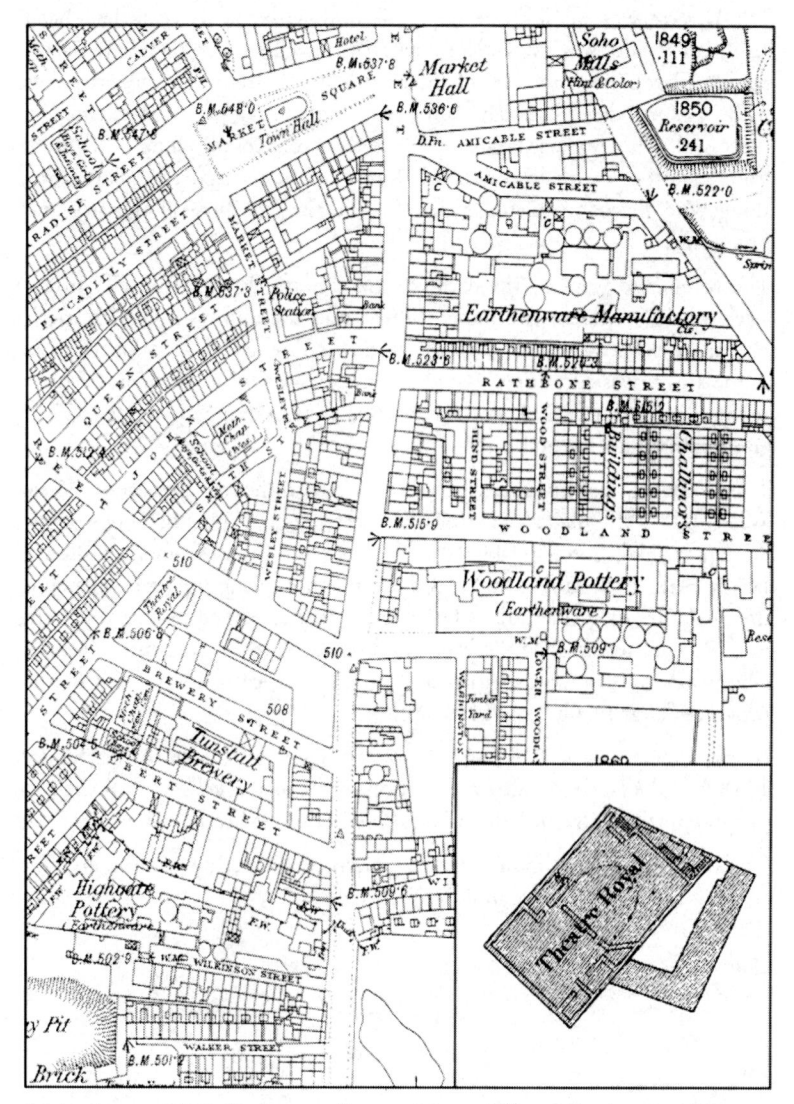

Main Image: 1882 Ordnance Survey Map of Tunstall, showing Theatre Royal roughly left of the centre.

Inset Image: Closeup of Theatre Royal, Tunstall showing internal structure and layout.

11

The theatre was up for sale in 1871, and within two years had been refurbished and was available to rent by travelling companies for £5 a week[10]. Throughout the rest of the decade it was frequently advertised as such, a sure sign that the venue was not proving to be financially successful. This was perhaps due to the difficulty in travelling to Tunstall from the other towns in the days before a public transport infrastructure, along with the competition from other theatres in Burslem, Hanley and Longton[11].

The venue also went by the name of the 'Theatre Royal, Tunstall'. In the week of 17th March 1873 the theatre was presenting Mlle. Beatrice's celebrated comedy drama 'Nos Intimes/Our Friends'. Like other theatres in the area it was occasionally used as a meeting hall; Dr. Kenealy, barrister at the longest trial in English legal history, appeared in September 1877 to give a talk on his life and career.

The building continued to pass between different managers; Jessie Westcott was the manager in 1876[12], before passing into the hands of the St. James' Hall company by 1879[13]. The building was renamed the St. James' Hall at the same time. It is doubtful that this group were related to the St. James Hall, Piccadilly. There was a further change of management in 1881 who refurbished the venue and renamed it the St. James' Theatre, advertised as "the most elegant and complete theatre for its size in the provinces"[14]. It finally closed in 1882.

In the same year, the building was sold to 'General' Booth for just under £2,000 and converted into a Salvation Army barracks[15]. It fulfilled this purpose until 1998 when the Salvation Army moved to new premises.

The building is now home to P. K. Ceramics, a catering wholesalers, but remains the oldest theatre building in the city.

Poynter's New Theatre, Burslem

Mr. Poynter opened, or reopened this theatre in Waterloo Road on 22nd December 1835. Illumination was by gas and the act drop showed a scene of Burslem Market Place, with "good fires" provided for heating. Opening night consisted of the melodrama 'Bottle Imp; or the Fiend and Sorcerer', with admittance to the pit charged at 1s. and the gallery at 6d. A flyer has survived in the scrapbooks of Enoch Wood, currently held by Stoke-on-Trent Museums, however there is no mention in the Staffordshire Advertiser of the time. It is likely that this was one of many travelling theatres passing through the area at the time, and possibly operated by theatre manager Chapman Poynter[16].

Snape's Theatre, Burslem

John Snape was one of the first men to bring theatre to the area. He originally came from Cheshire and was operating a travelling canvas theatre by 1850[17]. He passed through several towns in the area, particularly Burslem, in the 1840s and 50s. Snape's theatre appears to have attracted the wrong sort of audience; in 1870 Joseph Baggaley, a fourteen year old boy, stabbed twelve year old Martin Grogan at the venue, leaving him with a wound an inch and a half deep[18].

In 1871 Snape was operating the Lyceum Theatre in Burslem, built of wood and canvas and located on the recreation ground[19]. On 7th July 1872 a great storm hit the area, causing the building to be was struck by lightning and igniting the canvas roof. Little of the building was left standing after the ensuing blaze[20]. Snape quickly erected a temporary building, reopening with a production of 'The Forests of Bondy'[21]. A clue to the dimensions of Snape's travelling canvas theatre can be found in the following advert from *The Era* in October 1891:

> "Wanted, to Sell, Canvas Tilt, with rings to lace down. Fit Booth. 84ft long; 36 to 40ft wide. £6. J.W. Snape, Theatre, Garston"[22]

At some point son John William Snape took over the running of the theatre from his father. John William himself was born in Burslem in 1849 during his father's travels through the area. J. W. Snape returned to Burslem in 1877[23] and again in 1880 with a travelling theatre called the 'Royal Britannia' set up in Moorland Road[24].

In May 1881 he reapplied for a license to operate his travelling theatre in the town. The Wesleyans at Swan Bank objected to the application, complained that Snape's venue was too close to the chapel, to which he responded by offering to relocate. The theatre was reportedly very popular, causing children to stay out late at night and giving publicans cause to complain that their business was injured by its arrival[25].

A group of striking pottery workers met at Snape's Royal Britannia Theatre in November 1881[26]. One of the observers was a young Arnold Bennett, who later put this event into Clayhanger where Edwin and Hilda visited the meeting[27]. In Bennett's work Snape became Snagg, and his "Blood Tub" was located opposite the police station in Bursley.

This was the same position that Snape's later theatre, and subsequently the Wedgwood Theatre, occupied in Burslem. The following extract from *Clayhanger* describes the venue:

> "The Blood Tub, otherwise known as Snagg's, was the centre of nocturnal pleasure in Bursley. It stood almost on the very spot where the jawbone of a whale had once lain, as a supreme natural curiosity. It represented the softened manners which had developed out of the old medievalism of the century. It had supplanted the bear-pit and the cock-pit."

> "This last was a theatre with wooden sides and a canvas roof, and it would hold quite a crowd of people. In front of it was a platform, and an orchestra, lighted by oil flares that, as Big James and Edwin approached, were gaining strength in the twilight."

Snape seems to have opened a new, more permanent theatre in the town, the 'New Britannia' by the following year, seating 1,500[28]. One play presented in June 1882 was 'East Lynne' with Osborne Keane, Arthur Barry, John Glendinning and Moya Dean[29]. Snape appointed Hal Stoddard as manager to run the theatre during this period.

The theatre lasted until 1884 when Snape sold the building to 'The Salvation Mission' for a grand total of £250. The religious group was formed by former Salvation Army members including Rodney "Gipsy" Smith. The building was adapted for worship with the stage raised and enclosed, and narrow pointed windows fitted into the walls. As a chapel it could seat 1,300. It opened on Thursday 17th April 1884 with a service by Smith, followed by a brass band procession through the streets of Burslem [30]. Snape auctioned off the theatre contents the following Monday with "no reasonable offer refused". The building ceased to be used as a mission by 1896[31].

Snape returned to touring with his theatrical family, however he was back operating from a new building in Burslem by October 1887[32]. The building, called simply 'Snape's Theatre,' was located in Wedgwood Place. On this, his final residency in the town, he presented such delights as 'Fun On the Bristol, or a Night At Sea', 'Woman's Wit or, Scenes of the Indian Mutiny', and 'Orange Girl or, The Logan Stone and the Frozen Tarn'[33]. The following week, beginning Monday 31st October 1887, he presented a series of benefit nights for his family members with pieces including 'Lady Godiva', 'Bear Hunters' and the intriguingly titled 'Wanted, 1,000 Young Lady Painters for the Pot Works'[34].

Judging by reviews and classified adverts in trade paper *The Era*, Snape had left Burslem by 1888 and continued touring with the Royal Britannia, visiting Cradley Heath in 1888 and Crewe in 1891[35].

Old Theatres in the Potteries

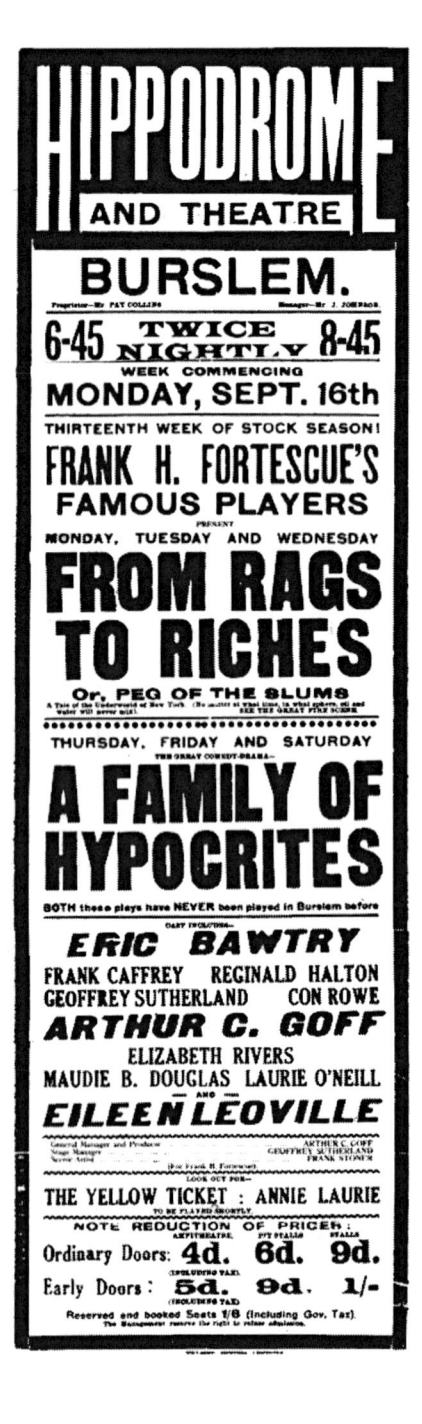

Wedgwood Theatre, Burslem

The Wedgwood Theatre originally stood between Wedgwood Street, Jenkins Street, and Price Street in Burslem.

The theatre opened on Monday 27th January 1896, operated by Basil Stuart and Matthew Hall[36]. The wooden building was designed by George Francis with construction work by both W. Brindley and F. Bettany, the latter the town surveyor at the time. 2,000 patrons were held in an auditorium on one level filled with wooden benches, divided into stalls and gallery by a wooden partition[37]. The stage measured 45ft wide by 40ft deep with a proscenium opening of around 20ft, and was fitted with "the latest patented appliances." The construction work on the venue was not complete come opening night however more than enough had occurred for performances to take place.

On the opening night, the mayor of Burslem took to the stage with the managers to proclaim the theatre open, announcing that he "hoped it would be a source of much pleasure to the inhabitants of the district". Various Burslem aldermen were also present at the event. Following the national anthem manager Matthew Hall promised that he "would be able to get some of the finest companies at Burslem".

After the formalities were complete the curtain was dropped and the orchestra commenced the overture to the night's opening performance of 'Maritana', a popular opera of the day. The performance by Mr. Nelson's English Opera Company was reported to be "altogether pleasing to a degree quite inexperienced." Shortly after opening further work was carried out on the theatre, including the festooning of the private boxes with drapery[38].

Material staged during the first few months included two pantomimes, an appearance of actor Charles Melville, and a production of Oscar Wilde's 'A Woman of No Importance'.

Left. Advertisement poster for Frank H. Fortescue's Famous Players at the Burslem Hippodrome and Theatre. Week commencing Monday 16th September 1929.

Old Theatres in the Potteries

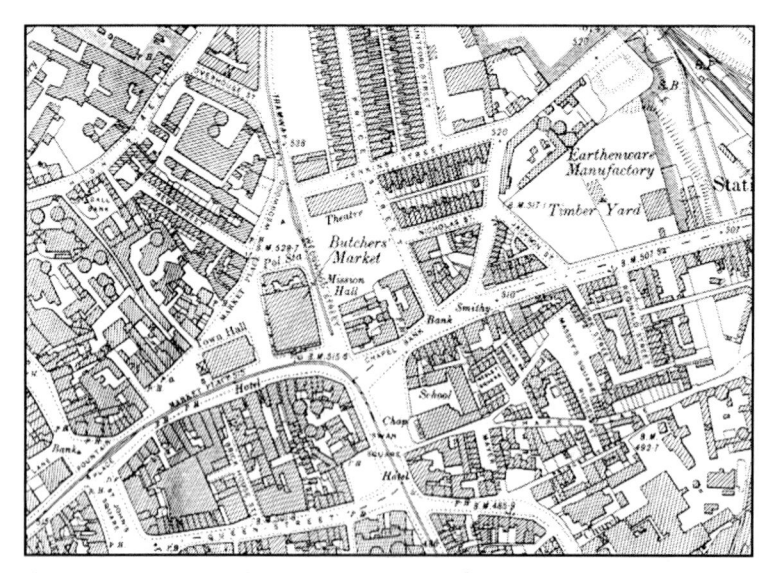

Above Image. 1898 Ordnance Survey Map of Burslem Town Centre. The Wedgwood Theatre can be clearly seen on the corner of Wedgwood Place and Jenkins Street. *Below.* 1925 Ordnance Survey Map. The Hippodrome can be seen in its new position next to the printing works. The dimensions of the building are the same.

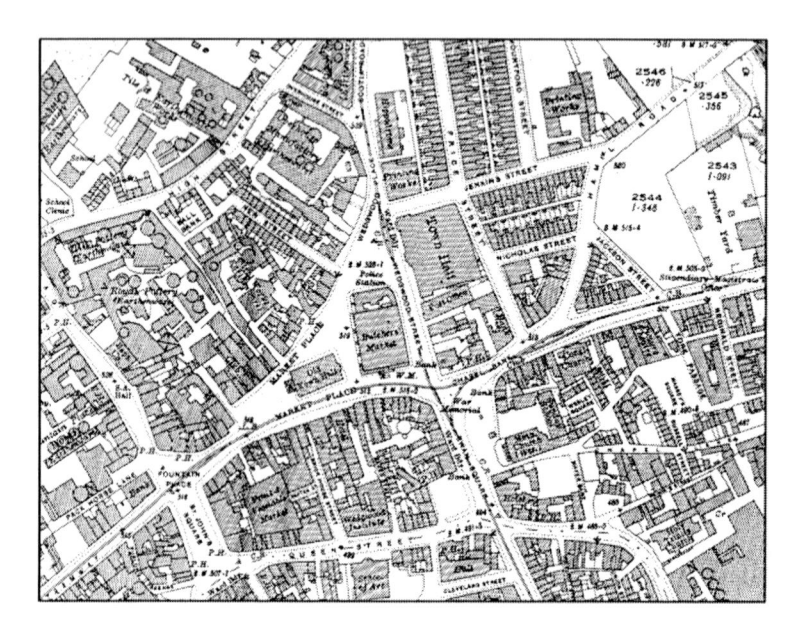

The theatre changed its name to the Hippodrome in Autumn 1907, operated at the time by C. Hamilton Baines[39]. At around the same time the theatre was dismantled and rebuilt on a site to the north of Warwick Savage's printing works[40].

The Hippodrome often presented silent films as part of the entertainments. By 1911, the theatre's programme alternated between programmes of silent film shorts interspersed with vaudeville acts and full stage productions such as 'The New Frivolity' – a musical comedy[41].

Pat Collins took over the building sometime after 1916 and operated a programme of variety between the two world wars[42]. In the week of Monday 16th February 1931 the theatre presented twice-nightly "The Most Wonderful Attraction ever seen in Burslem – Star Cabaret and Variety Road Show", including "the world's greatest xylophonist and master musician" V. M. Gaston, with Gertrude Ross "the famous pianiste", along with Monica Gold - "the versatile girl". In its later years before closure in the early 1940s it was operating as a cinema.

After several years standing empty, the Hippodrome in Burslem was dismantled on behalf of Pat Collins' widow at the end of 1947[43].

Above. The exterior of the Queen's Theatre, Burslem, facing onto Wedgwood Place.

Queen's Theatre, Burslem

The Queen's Hall was opened in 1911 as part of the new Burslem Town Hall, the third built in the town. The foundation stone was laid on 14th March 1910 and was built on the site of the relocated Wedgwood Theatre. A competition had been held to choose a design for the new hall, with the winning entry coming from architects Russell and Cooper.

The building was constructed with an eye to having Burslem becoming the civic centre of the new federated borough, however Stoke-upon-Trent eventually fulfilled this function. The new building included a large concert hall along the lines of other municipal venues, including the Victoria Hall in Hanley and the Free Trade Hall in Manchester. As such, it was not built for theatrical purposes[44]. Many concerts and dances were held in the hall and held film shows in its early years[45].

With the Theatre Royal looking set to close its doors completely to theatrical productions in the mid sixties, the council held discussions with the local amateur societies and scout groups with a view to adapting the Queen's Hall to become a theatre capable of staging large-scale musicals. This gained a pressing urgency in late 1966 when Mecca ceased offering the stage of the Theatre Royal for theatrical use.

A report from the City Architect was obtained. The stage was only 18ft 6in deep with 12ft of additional apron stage projecting into the auditorium. Minimal wing space was available, with no facilities for flying scenery and no ability to incorporate this into the stage house. The hall could hold 1,322, with 680 on the ground floor and 642 in the horseshoe shaped balcony. However with some seats 86ft from the stage and no rake on the ground floor, views were often blocked by other patrons and were said to lack intimacy. The side of the balcony also offered poor sight lines. All in all the building was not an ideal proposition for a theatre[46].

With very few options available to the council regarding live theatre in the city, the hall became the Queen's Theatre and was the home of the local amateur groups for many years, including the North Staffordshire Amateur Operatic and Dramatic Society, who took up residence here.

Old Theatres in the Potteries

QUEEN'S HALL, BURSLEM.

THURSDAY, FEBRUARY 2nd,

at 8.

FIRST VISIT TO THE DISTRICT OF

HENRY HOLST

THE FAMOUS DANISH VIOLINIST & LATE LEADER OF THE BERLIN PHILHARMONIC ORCHESTRA

The Copenhagen "Social Demokraten" says : "We place Mr. Henry Holst amongst the very best of our present day violin virtuosos"

with

JOHN BRENNAN

THE BRILLIANT CONCERT & BROADCAST PIANIST

The "Manchester Guardian" says : "By far the most distinguished feature of the evening, was the pianoforte playing of Mr. John Brennan." "Has ripened into an artist of high rank."

Seats Reserved at
WATSON'S, High Street, Hanley. 'Phone 2079
or KNAPPER'S (behind Queen's Hall), Burslem

BALCONY 3/- & 2/-, ARENA 1/-

Above. Handbill for a concert in the Queen's Hall, Burslem with Henry Holst and John Brennan. Monday 2nd February 1939.

The conversion work was paid for by the council, estimated as costing £6106 9s 9d. This included upgrading the stage amenities and electrical system, installing an intercom system and purchasing curtains and floor coverings[47].

Shows presented over the years by the amateur societies included 'Kiss Me Kate' (1969), 'The Sound of Music' (1970), 'Fiddler on the Roof' (1972), 'Madam Butterfly' (1973), 'The Card' (1974) and 'Chicago' (1983).

The theatre launched the careers of Jonathan Wilkes and his friend Robert Williams in the North Staffs. Amateur Operatic and Dramatic Society's production of 'Hans Andersen' in 1985. Three years later Williams played the 'Artful Dodger' in the same society's production of Lionel Bart's 'Oliver!'. Footage of this performance often makes its way into television shows on Williams' life[48].

The building was poorly maintained over the years despite it becoming a listed building in 1972. As a result the theatre closed in 1998 for safety reasons, with part of the ceiling collapsing a year later. Urgent remedial works were subsequently forced to take place.

After lying empty for several years a 99 year lease was obtained by Steve Ball, and the Queen's Theatre Production Society currently operate and maintain the building as a concert venue and theatre without monetary assistance from the council. In order to improve the views a bleacher unit has been installed, giving raked ground floor seating leading up to the balcony[49]. The theatre generally presents a mixture of concerts and amateur productions.

Above. Illustration of the Coliseum Theatre of Varieties, Burslem.

Coliseum Theatre of Varieties, Burslem

The Coliseum was located on Bournes Bank, Burslem, and was opened in 1914.

The theatre was built to the designs of Wood and Goldstraw of Hanley and Tunstall, with construction by P. Pemberton of Tunstall. The entrance to the building was contained in a Corinthian columned portico facing onto Bournes Bank, and above the entrance stood a tower topped with a globe, similar to that above the London Coliseum.

The auditorium was constructed to hold around 1,790 patrons over the stalls and large circle, as well as the boxes around the rear of the theatre. Electric light was installed, with "handsome pendants" to reflect the light. The upholstery, and proscenium drapes were of a crimson colour[50] with "tasteful and handsome" plaster mouldings adorning the walls and balcony. The stage was 26ft deep with a 32ft wide proscenium opening, fitted with an asbestos curtain. Hanging above were the Burslem coat of arms, said to be in their "proper colours."[51]

It was the intention of the management, "local gentlemen" including Harold Hales, to install beneath the stage an entertainment facility comprising of a billiard hall, refreshment rooms and a "live target" game, where patrons could practise their shooting on projected targets. It is unknown as to whether this venture ever came to fruition.

It was planned that the theatre would present a film show in the afternoons, with two variety shows in the evening filled with "first-class talent". Opening night came on Monday 16th November 1914. The festivities began with Mrs. Margaret Dempsey performing the national anthem before councillor J.H. Edwards, chairman of the watch committee, proposed a vote of confidence to the management[52].

The night's acts included the Dempsey-Ackyroyd Trio, comprising of a singer, violinist and flautist, comedian Tom Seymour, dancer Harris Coonie and ventriloquist Norman Osbourne. Motion pictures showing the opening of parliament were also included, all accompanied by the orchestra under the hand of Mr. R. Ross. At the time of opening the manager was Mr. B Bown.

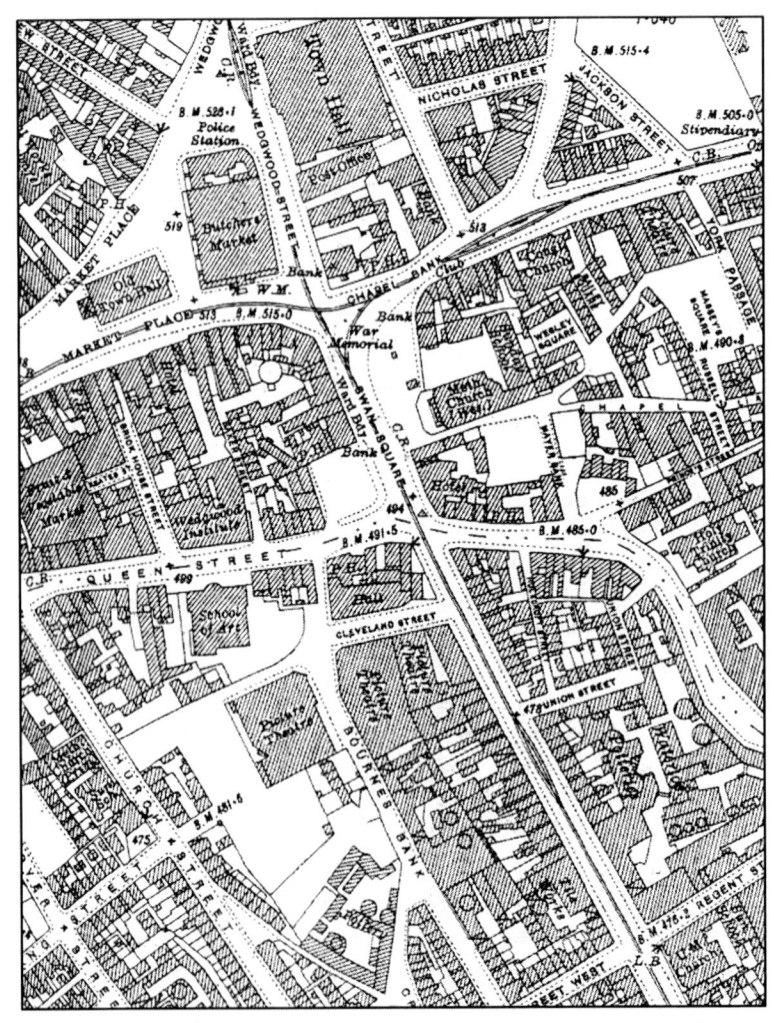

Below. 1925 Ordnance Survey map of Burslem. Three picture theatres were located around Cleveland Street and Bournes Bank. The Coliseum is to the west of the two others, the Palace and the Palladium.

Although built as a variety theatre, operas were a frequent visitor from the time of its opening, albeit in English. These included 'Maritana', 'Daughter of the Regiment', 'Bohemian Girl' and 'Il Trovatore'.

One stage production of note at this time was 'Damaged Lives'. Starring Mr. and Mrs. F. Dudman Bromwich, it was a story concerning the life and relationships of potter Jim Bannister. It possessed a unique feature in that the stage action frequently cut to "cinematograph pictures of stirring episodes in the streets of Burslem." Its initial one-week run in September 1917 was so popular that it forced a revival just two months later. The audiences were said to be "greatly stirred up" by seeing their home town on the big screen[53].

A twice-nightly variety bill for the week of 10th December 1917 included "The World's Greatest Conjurer" Chung Ling Soo with his assistant Miss Suee Seen, Cissie Cueette the "quaint character comedienne", Thornbury "the comedy cartoonist and lightning painter", Coquelli – "the man who tickles the world" and Arthur Slater – "the whistling man in white"[54].

Already declining in popularity at the time of opening, the live acts were replaced within a few years to become a full-time cinema towards the end of the 1910s. Passing through the hands of the Biocolor circuit, it was purchased by the Gaumont British chain in 1929 who commenced a refurbishment project. This including the installation of a Compton theatre organ beneath the stage and Western Electric Sound, reopening 14th July 1930, with 'The Sap' and 'The Two Big Vagabonds'.

Cinemascope was installed early in 1955 at which point the organ was removed. The building was renovated further in May 1955 with the facade modernised and auditorium redecorated, the venue being renamed the 'Gaumont' at the same time[55]. The cinema continued operating until 12th November 1960 when it closed with a performance of 'Too Many Crooks'. The building was subsequently demolished.

Old Theatres in the Potteries

Theatre Royal, Hanley

The Theatre Royal, Hanley was the principal theatre in the area for many years and has a very long and varied history.

In 1835 the Primitive Methodists, previously housed in a chapel in Stafford Row, moved to a new chapel in Brunswick Street holding 450[56]. The chapel possessed a sunday school to accommodate 141 pupils[57]. The land where the chapel stood was called 'Brick Kiln Fields', once part of Viscount Granville's colliery[58].

After the methodists moved into a new chapel on the junction of Marsh Street and Brunswick Street, occupier Thomas Bundred let the building to a group of around 80 working men at a "moderate" price[59]. It was thus modified and reconstructed into the 'People's Hall', the purpose of which was to provide lectures and public meetings to the working class of the area to improve them for the greater good. Around 900 people could be accommodated in the hall, with 450 in both the gallery and ground floor. The majority of the shareholders were said to be "democratic", and would not allow immoral or drunken acts to occur in the building.

The hall opened on Monday 29th April 1850 with guests at that opening including Mr. O'Connor, MP, who told the assembled crowd to adhere to the "Charter, and no surrender!"[60]. Those running the hall were said to be sympathetic to the chartist agenda.

An example of the events at the People's Hall can be seen on Sunday 9th March 1850 when Samuel Philips Day, a former monk of the order of the Presentation, lectured on "The March of the Mind" and "Romanism The Religion of Terror, Historically Considered". Admission would cost 3d in the gallery and 2d. on the ground floor[61].

A grand tea party was held to celebrate the first anniversary of the hall, where it was announced that it was the intention of the directors to open a library at the hall and to continue raising the money for the purchase of the theatre from the Methodists[62].

This hall for the working man cannot have been much of a success as towards the end of 1851 Messrs. Bamford and Green, local pottery manufacturers, began to present temperance pieces in the hall. These short plays exhibited "the evils of drunkenness, and the benefit of abstaining altogether from intoxicating drinks." These soon developed into other dramatic works, all presented illegally without a license.

The venue was brought to the attention of the local constabulary who observed that the audience comprised largely of disorderly young men and women, partaking in smoking and drinking. Prostitutes and their "bullies" were also seen on the premises.

On 21st January 1852 Bamford and Green applied for a theatrical licence at special sessions in Longton, which was refused by the magistrates by a majority of four to one. Several reasons were given. The report from the police inspector played a large part, along with the fact that the Newcastle and Pottery Theatre was only two miles away. Magistrate T. B. Rose commented "the licensing of another theatre in the neighbourhood would be an evil". At the same meeting another application from Stephen Pickhull was due to be put forward, subsequently withdrawn following their first refusal[63].

Despite this initial setback, others saw potential in a conversion of the People's Hall for theatrical purposes. Both James Rogers, manager of theatres at Newcastle, Lichfield and Stafford, and William Shuker Thorne, the proprietor of a travelling theatre, applied for a licence. Despite it being the opinion of some the magistrates that a theatre was not necessary in the area, a licence was granted to Rogers on a trial basis for six months during the licensing session at the Trentham Inn on 31st August 1852. This was due largely to Rogers' previous experience and good character, proved by the production of several written testimonials[64].

Rogers announced that he would be spending a "considerable sum of money" to convert the People's Hall into a theatre[65]. Construction work was started, carried out by Mr. Bedson to the designs of John Caunt. This involved the installation of side and centre boxes, decorated "a la boudoir", and a gallery rising from the ground floor in the style of an amphitheatre. Gas-light was installed, with scenery by Messrs. Rowe and Gordon and a drop cloth was painted by Robert Dearlove.

Thursday 25th November 1852 was opening night of the new 'Royal Pottery Theatre', in the week following the funeral of the Duke of Wellington. Three items were on the bill – 'The Cavalier!', 'Time Tries All', and 'Wilful Murder!', a farce[66]. As was standard with these occasions the company performed a rendition of the national anthem beforehand. Performances played twice-nightly, at 7.30pm and 9pm, with a centre box costing 2s, side boxes 1s and the gallery 6d. Adverts boasted that the theatre would be presenting "Singing and Dancing; to be followed with laughable farces and dramas."

That first few weeks certainly showed a range of performances; plays like 'Uncle Tom's Cabin' and the melodrama of 'The Tragedy of Jane Shore' were followed by an engagement of Monsieur Desaris and his highly-trained dogs and monkeys[67], quite a contrast!

The building was not used exclusively for dramatic purposes; in an advert in *The Era* newspaper in 1854 the 'Royal Pottery Theatre' was advertised as being available for "Concerts, Lectures and Entertainments &c."[68]

In August 1856 Rogers relinquished the management and sub-let the theatre to manager Richard Samuel Thorne at £5 a week for 20 weeks. He soon dropped the prices with the lowest price ticket costing 3d., which attracted a much younger clientele. The theatre gained a reputation for "demoralising scenes"; smoking, drinking, cursing, and fighting were reported to regularly take place inside. Large crowds would gather outside the venue, disrupting those living in Brunswick Street. On one occasion, two boys in the audience leapt up onto the stage and had a "set-to". Thorne was fined £5 for operating the theatre without a license, although according to the sub-inspector of police Thorne was rarely at the theatre.

The final straw seems to have come with the sighting of prostitutes plying their trade in the auditorium. On Tuesday 23rd December 1856 those in charge at the Keele Petty Sessions refused Thorne's application for the renewal of the operating licence, so as "not to inflict upon the townships of Hanley and Shelton so great an evil"[69]. The theatre subsequently closed.

Thomas Rogers soon returned, attempting regain his license. He met with the magistrates in May, assuring them that the previous problems would not recur and that the building would be "thoroughly renovated". This application was dismissed until the new corporation of Hanley came into being[70].

Development of the Theatre Royal, Hanley

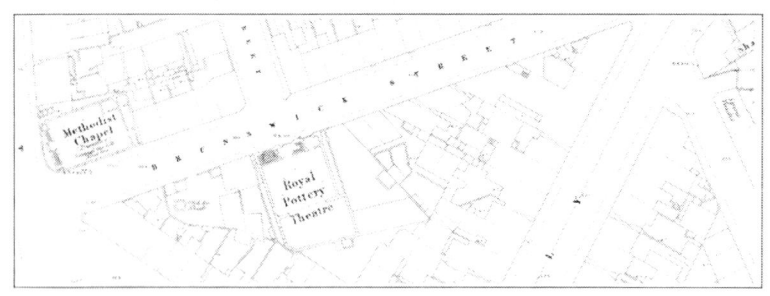

Above. The Royal Pottery Theatre in 1865, following the 1857 reconstruction.

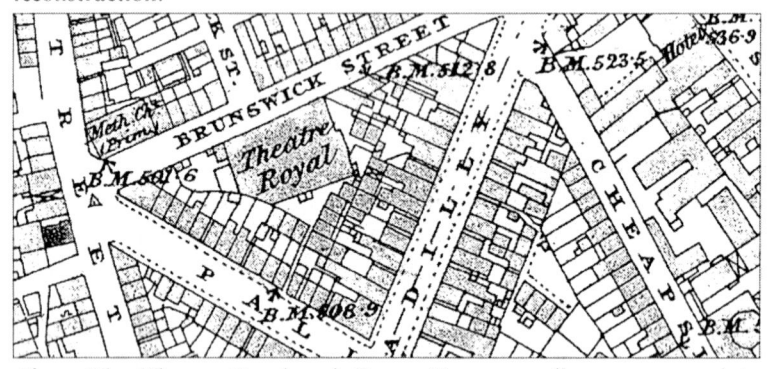

Above. The Theatre Royal and Opera House, totally reconstructed in 1871. The auditorium runs parallel to Brunswick Street. 1879.

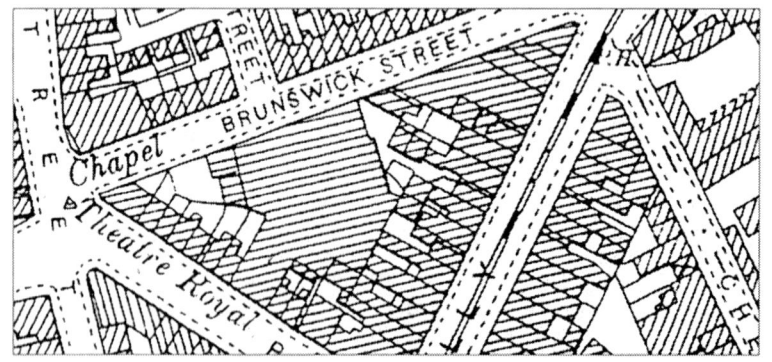

Above. The Theatre Royal in 1898, following both the 1887 and 1894 rebuilds. The auditorium now runs perpendicular to Brunswick Street with an entrance onto Pall Mall.

In the mean time Rogers set about the promised reconstruction work on the Royal Pottery Theatre. The building was gutted internally and extended southwards to create a new stage area[71]. A new interior was constructed comprising of a ground floor pit with promenade, boxes with promenade and a gallery. The auditorium was now 35ft deep and could hold 1,400 persons. The stage measured 46ft wide by around 25ft deep, with a proscenium opening of 25ft. A new facade was constructed facing Brunswick Street, built of brick and cement in the Corinthian style. The entire building measured 55ft by 75ft. The architect for the works was T. E. Shaw of Hanley with the building work by builder John Jones. The total construction cost was reported as £500[72].

Tired of waiting until the incorporation of Hanley and Shelton was complete, Rogers impatiently applied at Newcastle's Guildhall for a license on 6th July 1857 and was awarded with one for twelve months. The magistrates were satisfied with Rogers' track record and the standard of the building work[73]. It was noted that given that a license was granted to Matthew Wardhaugh's 'Royal Alma Theatre' in Longton, there should be no reason to oppose one for the Hanley theatre.

The 'Royal Pottery Theatre' reopened on Saturday 1st August 1857 for Wakes week with a "good company of performers", before closing again on the 12th for the continuation of the refurbishment works. It finally reopened on Saturday 22nd August[74].

Despite the works, some critics felt that the theatre should bring itself upmarket by banning smoking and by separating the centre boxes from the side boxes, which the critic from the *Birmingham Daily Post* felt would attract "a large number of fastidious persons"[75].

Mr. Gustavus Vaughan Brooke, Mademoiselle Beatrice, and Mr James Elphinstone - the "celebrated London actor"[76], all appeared on stage in the 1860s. Typical fare included melodramas such as 'The Life of a Pottery Lass' by Mr. Walters, performed on 9th March 1870, and 'Belphegor'. During a production of this in 1865, actor Elliot Graham was severely injured when crockery thrown as part of the play bounced off the proscenium and hit him in the face, leaving him with a cut severe enough to force him out of the play[77].

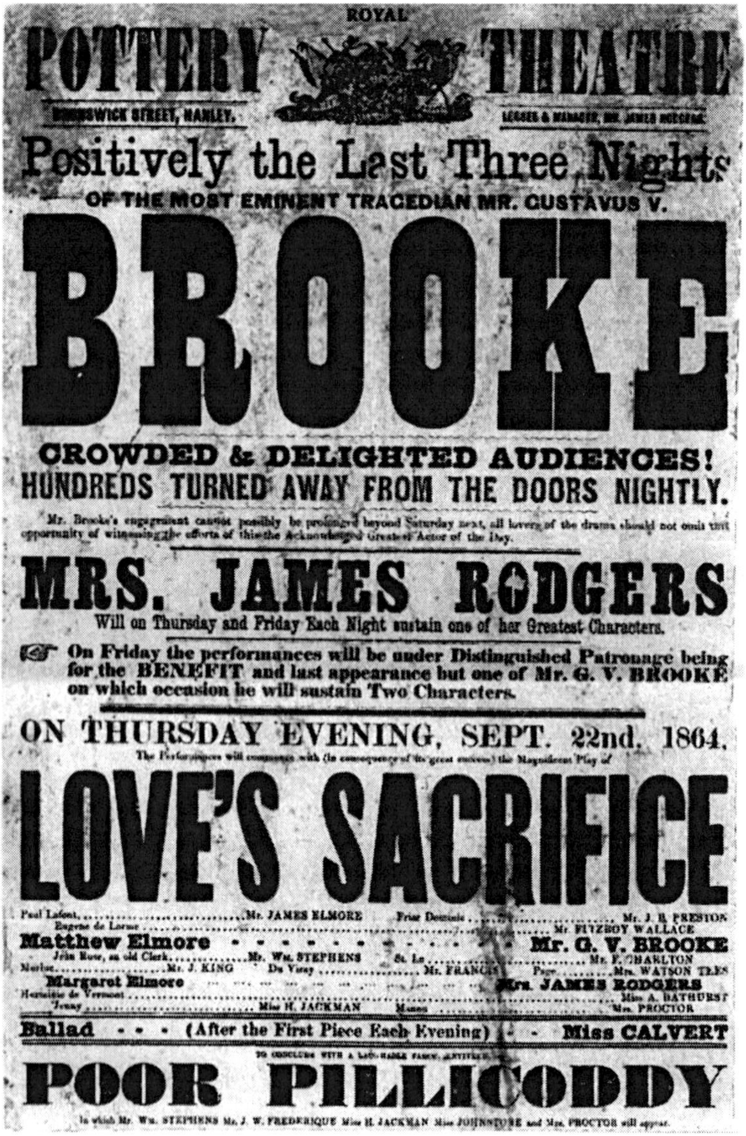

ROYAL
POTTERY THEATRE
BRUNSWICK STREET, HANLEY.
Positively the Last Three Nights
OF THE MOST EMINENT TRAGEDIAN MR. GUSTAVUS V.
BROOKE
CROWDED & DELIGHTED AUDIENCES!
HUNDREDS TURNED AWAY FROM THE DOORS NIGHTLY.
Mr. Brooke's engagement cannot possibly be prolonged beyond Saturday next, all lovers of the drama should not omit this opportunity of witnessing the efforts of this the Acknowledged Greatest Actor of the Day.
MRS. JAMES RODGERS
Will on Thursday and Friday Each Night sustain one of her Greatest Characters.
On Friday the performances will be under Distinguished Patronage being for the BENEFIT and last appearance but one of Mr. G. V. BROOKE on which occasion he will sustain Two Characters.
ON THURSDAY EVENING, SEPT. 22nd. 1864.
LOVE'S SACRIFICE
Paul Lafont .... Mr. JAMES ELMORE
Friar Dominic .... Mr. J. B. PRESTON
Eugene de Lorme .... Mr. FITZROY WALLACE
Matthew Elmore .... Mr. G. V. BROOKE
John Rowe, an old Clerk .... Mr. Wm. STEPHENS
St. Lo .... Mr. F. CHARLTON
Morlac .... Mr. J. KING
Du Vinoy .... Mr. FRANCIS
Page .... Mrs. WATSON TEES
Margaret Elmore .... Mrs. JAMES RODGERS
Hermine de Vermont .... Miss A. BATHURST
Jenny .... Miss H. JACKMAN
Manon .... Mrs. PROCTOR
Ballad - - - (After the First Piece Each Evening) - - Miss CALVERT
TO CONCLUDE WITH A LAUGHABLE FARCE, ENTITLED
POOR PILLICODDY
In which Mr. Wm. STEPHENS Mr. J. W. FREDERIQUE Miss H. JACKMAN Miss JOHNSTONE and Mrs. PROCTOR will appear.

Above and left. Advertising poster for the Royal Pottery Theatre, starring Gustavus V. Brooke. September 1864.

In the middle of 1870 the theatre closed for rebuilding. The original Royal Pottery Theatre was said to be "dingy and inconvenient" and "unfit" for the size of district it served[78]. Competition had also arisen from the newer and better appointed Prince of Wales Theatre in Tunstall and Royal Victoria Theatre in Longton. The whole site was demolished and after eight months of construction, the new Theatre Royal and Opera House was complete[79].

The architect of the new building was proprietor Thomas Hinde, and construction completed by R. Twemlow. The frontage faced Brunswick Street for 104 feet and was built of brick in the Corinthian style. Pilasters of white brick with stone capitals adorned the facade, topped with a cornice. This can still be seen in Brunswick Street today with some later modifications.

Much was made in the local press of the improved fire provisions, with almost five times the amount of fire exits compared to the old building, allowing the building to be emptied in three minutes[80]. An iron curtain and an on-site water hose were also installed. During this period, theatrical fires were common due to the high flammability of the materials on stage and the use of 'limelight' for stage illumination, utilising a highly explosive mix of hydrogen and oxygen.

The new building ran parallel to Brunswick Street and the stage was sited to the east side of the site[81], measuring 43ft deep and 54ft wide. Every facility was said to be afforded for the painting, arrangement and change of scenery, with flying machinery installed for the scene changes. A dropcloth of "Modern Italy" in the style of Turner hung on the stage, painted by R.M Hyde. Seven dressing rooms were provided for the artists along with a green room. The auditorium could seat 3,200 split over pit, gallery, and two tiers of boxes. Adjacent to the theatre were refreshment rooms for the use of the patrons.

Above. The facade of the Theatre Royal and Opera House facing Brunswick Street, built in 1871. It became the stage wall with the 1887 rebuild and survived the fire in 1949. It currently houses entrances to the nightclubs operating in the building.

The cost of the construction given at the time was £4,500. The first performance in the new venue was given on Monday 6th March 1871 of both "Leah" and Craven's "Checkmate". The star was Mrs. Rodgers, the wife of the manager. Following the interval, the company appeared on stage and sang the national anthem before manager James Rodgers gave an address, proclaiming that:

> "no money – ne exertions shall be spared on my part to give you the very best entertainment that can possibly be provided."

In 1872 James H. Elphinstone, who had previously visited the theatre as a touring actor, became manager. This was a position that he and his sons would hold for many decades to come[82]. He was previously the proprietor of the Royal Pavilion in London and "lost a fortune" after it burned down and the safe stolen in 1856[83].

A week's playbill at the Theatre Royal in 1874 advertised a double bill of 'Hearts Delight' - an adaptation of Dickens' Dombey and Son, and 'Fra Diavolo! or Beauty and the Brigands', with 'Sithors to Grind' joining them on the Friday. Top seats costing 2s 6d in the dress circle[84].

In 1884 twelve year old Richard Ford was charged with disorderly conduct at the Borough Police Court, after persistently throwing ginger beer bottles from the gallery of the Theatre Royal down into the pit. No one appears to have been hurt by his actions however he was fined 5s 6d. plus costs[85].

By the mid 1880s, the theatre was once again proving to be inadequate. Although the competition from the Tunstall theatre had ceased following its purchase by the Salvation Army, a group of businessmen in Longton were planning to construct a bigger and better theatre which would become the Queen's. Lessee Elphinstone, together with his manager son Charles, obtained plans for a new theatre from Charles J. Phipps and Frank Matcham. Both were renowned theatrical architects, with many of their theatres still in use to this day.

THEATRE ROYAL,
HANLEY.

Sole Lessee and Manager — Mr. JAMES ELPHINSTONE

Engagement at an enormous Expense,

FOR SIX NIGHTS ONLY,
OF THE

LONDON COMPANY

Under the Direction of

MR. ALFRED YOUNG,

Specially organized for the Performances, in the Provinces, of Mr. ANDREW HALLIDAY's Great Success,

HEART'S DELIGHT

Which has, for the last Six Months, been acted at the Globe Theatre, London, to crowded and enthusiastic audiences.

Mr. ELPHINSTONE has great pleasure in drawing the attention of his patrons to this engagement with Mr. ALFRED YOUNG, who so successfully produced

MISS CHESTER

In Hanley last season.

Mr. YOUNG having secured the sole provincial right of Mr. HALLIDAY's Great "LONDON SUCCESS which will be presented, as nightly playing in London to crowded houses.

"Cheers, Tears, and Laughter."—*Punch*.

Above. Flyer for Theatre Royal from May 1874.

The construction work was put in the hands of Towles of Birmingham and J. Turner of Hanley, and took around five months. The existing theatre was gutted and rebuilt to become the stage and backstage area, with the old facade facing Brunswick Street becoming the rear wall of the stage. This measured 92ft in width and 46ft deep, laid out in 20 sections and fitted with 12 new dressing rooms for artistes[86]. A 18ft deep cellar allowed large set pieces to be raised from below with the fly tower allowing them to be flown in from above. These and other stage machinery would "permit the successful performance of spectacular plays so much in vogue" at the time, on the "most perfect stage in the provinces."[87]

The auditorium was housed in a new building constructed onto the south wall of the existing building. This was split over four levels. The pit could seat 1,100 and measured 56ft by 52ft, said to be a "great improvement"on the old[88]. The next level was the circle, holding around 250 in "easy chairs", then the upper circle holding around 250 in upholstered seats. The final level was the gallery, holding around 1,000 on wooden benches. This gave a total of around 2,600 patrons. These balconies were supported by iron pillars, obstructing the views from behind them, and each level had refreshment bars provided. Internal decoration was by Mr. Brunton of London with the decorative painting by Samuel Bateman. A dome was installed in the centre of the ceiling, in the centre of which was a 'gasolier'. Gas lighting was installed throughout the new building, which could be independently controlled. Facilities for an orchestra were provided with capacity for around 25 musicians in the pit, and the reconstruction work was said to cost £8,000.

By opening night the works had not been fully completed; the upholstered seats in the circle were yet to be installed and the entrances were still in Brunswick Street. However, the theatre was opened for the beginning of the local Wakes week so as not to miss out on the great deal of business it created. Work continued on the new entrance in Pall Mall which when completed gave access to the pit, boxes and lower circles. This entrance has survived, albeit with some aesthetic alterations, and can still be seen in Pall Mall. The gallery was still to be accessed from Brunswick Street following the work.

Opening night was on Monday 1st August 1887[89] where a production of 'The Crimes of Paris' was staged starring Charles Melville[90]. A ticket would have cost 2s in the lower circle, 1s in the upper circle, 8d in the pit, and 4d in the gallery.

An amusing incident happened at the theatre on Tuesday 24th April 1888 when a cow, being walked down Brunswick Street, ran through the stage door of the theatre and rampaged around the stage. It was only stopped when she found herself stuck head first in a window on the set. It was "not without difficulty" to remove the creature from its predicament[91].

James H. Elphinstone, head of the family and theatre owner, passed away in 1892. The theatre was put into chancery and purchased by his sons Charles and George[92].

Following this acquisition, the brothers set about a scheme of expansion which would later include the construction of a new variety theatre, the Grand. In June of 1894 the Theatre Royal was closed whilst "most elaborate and extensive" structural alterations were carried out on the building to the designs of Frank Matcham[93]. In just six weeks the theatre was reconstructed by a large number of contractors, headed by building firm Cornelius Cornes of Hanley[94].

The rear wall of the auditorium was removed and rebuilt around 9 feet closer to Piccadilly, allowing for extra seating including a dress circle double the size of the previous. Four new, elaborately decorated private boxes were constructed close to the stage and new plaster ornamentation was installed on the front of the balconies. The ceiling was repainted and the columns each side of the stage decorated with gold.

Electric lighting was fitted in the auditorium, said to be a "vast improvement on the gaslight." There was also a new heating system and new adjustable seats by Deans of Birmingham[95]. Seating was arranged with 75 in the orchestra stalls, 1,200 in the pit, 600 in the circle, 400 in the second circle, and 600 in the gallery, 2,875 in total[96]. A new iron and glass marquee was built over the main entrance and a vestibule constructed inside to reduce draughts into the auditorium. Backstage facilities were seemingly unaltered.

Above. The facade of the Theatre Royal facing Pall Mall, constructed in the 1887 rebuild. The illuminated sign was added in the 1920s.

Reopening night was on Monday, 6th August 1894, with another production of 'The Crimes of Paris', again starring Charles Melville. The new private boxes would cost £1 1s for the evening, a huge amount for the time. If they were less well-off, patrons could sit in the gallery, still accessed from Brunswick Street, for 3d, equivalent to a mere 75p now!

The Theatre Royal continued to play host to a mix of dramas and musical comedies, with such shows as 'The Queen's Shilling' (1896), 'Lolo – The New Comic Opera' (1900), 'Amorelle' (1904) and 'The Earl and the Girl' (1907). It also attracted some of the big names in theatre including William Greet, Ida Molesworth, Emma and Percy Hutchison, H.B. Irving and his wife Dorothea Beard. In 1904, the great Ellen Terry visited and starred in 'The Good Hope' and 'Much Ado about Nothing'. The D'Oyle Carte, Moody Manners and Carl Rosa opera companies were also frequent visitors, presenting such favourites as 'Tannhäuser', 'The Mikado', 'Faust' and 'The Merry Widow'[97]. Fortunately for the people of Hanley these were presented in English.

In 1900 George Elphinstone left the 'Hanley Theatres and Circus' company, whilst brother Charles continued as managing director[98]. Charles' son Douglas was later appointed manager before his untimely death in August 1909 at the age of 26[99]. Elphinstone retired in 1920, with the company assets sold off at the same time. Charles G.W. Elphinstone later passed away in 1931[100].

The new owners of the Royal were National Provincial Circuit Limited. They radically changed the bill at the venue, with shows now playing twice nightly without an interval. The manager was Albert Bulmer, sharing the role with an identical one at the nearby Grand on behalf of its new owners[101].

A small local syndicate under the title Potteries Theatres Ltd. purchased the theatre around eighteen months later, comprising of Arthur Birkett and his brother Edmund, Albert Bulmer, G.T. Devonshire, W. J. Moxon and secretary T.A. Grant[102]. Audiences were already dwindling with competition from cinema and shows were making substantial losses[103]. Manager Charles Bulmer told *The Stage* that conversion to a cinema was a real possibility unless audience figures increased. With this in mind a cinematograph licence was obtained and a lantern room constructed at the rear of the stage[104]. At least one film was shown however the venue fortunately remained as a venue for live theatre throughout the twenties and beyond.

THEATRE ROYAL
HANLEY, Stoke-on-Trent.

WEEK COMMENCING AUGUST 10th, 1931.

Evenings at 7-45.   Matinee Thursday at 2-30.

Extraordinary Attraction!

DON'T MISS SEEING

DICK TUBB

The Famous London Comedian

in

LORD BABS

London's Funniest Farcical Comedy
By KEBLE HOWARD

FROM THE

Vaudeville & Criterion Theatres,
LONDON, W.

The Laugh of a Lifetime

A. Taylor & Sons, Printers, Station Road, Wombwell.

Above. Handbill for comedy 'Lord Babs' at the Theatre Royal in 1931

Above. Poster for Variety at the Theatre Royal, April 1934

Theatre Royal

HANLEY
"The Potteries Own"

Proprietors
THE POTTERIES THEATRES LTD

Licensee
ARTHUR BIRKETT

General Manager
A. W. THOMPSON

Programme 2d.

Old Theatres in the Potteries

TWO HOUR!

Replatal service for all makes of car batteries at

H. W. Teeton Ltd.,
Foundry-St.,
HANLEY.

Exide

Telephone:
Stoke-on-Trent
2600

"CINDERELLA"

ALL STAR CAST INCLUDING

MARGARET MORGAN

PEGGY BEDELL

NANCY NEALE   MANLEY BROS.

JOE HUDSON   GERTRUDE CONCANNON

JOHNNY KAVANAGH

HARUM SCARUM GIRLS   PERCY PRYDE   THE KUTE KIDS

ELECTRIC FAIRY COACH DRAWN BY FOUR MINATURE PONIES.

Delightful Ballet   Beautiful Girls   Roars of Laughter

SPECIALITIES BY:
          THE MANLEY BROTHERS

The Royal Quartette.   The Harum Scarum Girls

The Kute Kids   Bessie Leslie's Doll Act

FRUIT FOR HEALTH!

FORSTER'S for FRUIT

(T. FORSTER & SONS)

| A Firm with a Record of 35 Years Trading. | MARKET HALL, HANLEY. Wednesday — Friday Saturday. | Choice Fruits at Lowest Market Prices. |

Above and Left. Programme for the 1936 pantomime Cinderella.

Old Theatres in the Potteries

Above. The facade of the Theatre Royal following the 1932 renovations.

In 1932, the facade of the theatre was modernised, with the Matcham brickwork rendered over and a new, art-deco marquee installed over the entrance[105]. Further improvements in the thirties included redecoration, reseating and improved cloakrooms, lounges and lavatories.

By this time the Theatre Royal had increased the amount of variety shows appearing whilst still presenting a mix of drama, operetta and musical comedy. In the week of 16th April 1934, George H. Elliot, Gertie Gitana, Ted Ray and Tubby Turner starred in an "All Star Variety Week" playing twice-nightly. The theatre had previously adopted the advertising slogan "The Potteries Own", which would stick for decades to come.

The theatre frequently played host to large musical comedies direct from their London runs. These included "Rose Marie" (1926) and "Mr Cinders" by Vivian Ellis (1929). The local amateur societies also frequently booked the theatre, with the North Staffs. Amateur Operatic Society presenting "The New Moon" by Sigmund Romberg in 1932, and the Stoke-on-Trent Amateur Operatic Society with "The Desert Song" in 1933.

Percy Hughes came to the Theatre Royal in October 1938 as manager, a position he would hold for the next twenty-three years[106].

The outbreak of war in 1939 initially closed entertainment venues but they were reopened quickly. Stars like Stanley Holloway[107] and Max Wall[108] performed at the theatre in an effort to persuade the people to 'Holiday at Home'. At Christmas 1939, the pantomime 'Red Riding Hood' was staged starring northern actress Betty Driver as Jill. Betty would later appear as barmaid Betty Turpin in Coronation Street. The national tour of London hit 'Me and My Girl' also visited in February 1940[109].

Not content with just playing their instruments, the orchestra of the theatre joined in with war work, with some working for upwards of eight hours a day in local munitions factories[110]. During the war years, several of the established companies moved out of London to escape the blitz and toured the provinces. An example of this came in March 1942 when the company of Old Vic presented Chekhov's 'The Cherry Orchard', starring Edith Evans and Athene Seyler[111].

During the war, the front of the theatre programmes gave the following notice giving advice in case of an air raid.

> "In the Event of AIR RAID WARNING being received during a performance you will be notified from the Stage, and the Show will go on.
>
> If you leave the Theatre, WALK – DON'T RUN to the Exit you have chosen"

Although the theatre did not succumb to an air raid, their printers Keates were hit, depriving the theatre of programmes for a time[112].

Following the war director of local bus company PMT Frederick Peake purchased the theatre at a cost of over £72,000, and planned a series of renovations to bring the theatre up-to-date[113]. The iron pillars supporting the balconies were to be replaced with cantilevers to give uninterrupted views and the electric system would also be overhauled. In 1949 rewiring was underway throughout the venue to cope with a switch to mains electricity, which would provide the extra power needed for the larger touring companies. It was previously generated in-house at a lower voltage.

Postwar, the theatre regularly presented both the Sadler's Wells Ballet and Opera companies, and also presented "The King Stag" by Carlo Gozzi, starring a young Hattie Jacques.

The Fire

Following a performance of 'Les Patineurs' by the Sadlers Wells Ballet on the night of Wednesday 1st June 1949, smoke could be smelt in the auditorium. After investigations no fire could be found but Hanley fire station were kept on alert.

At around 5am the next day, Thursday 2nd June, P.C. Till was on his beat in Marsh Street and noticed smoke rising from the roof of the theatre. He alerted the night watchman of the building who assured him that the auditorium was not alight. Climbing to the roof of the stage, they opened a hatch to the space above the stalls to be greeted by the sight of burning roof timbers. The fire brigade led by W. Smith B.E.M arrived on the scene within minutes. Upon entering the auditorium, burning beams were already falling onto the pit and stage[114]. Initially set up inside the building, the firemen evacuated before the roof collapsed into the stalls at around 6am, just one hour after the fire was first detected.

SWINNERTON'S
MILK BAR
PICCADILLY
HANLEY

Satisfaction or money back now as always

AT

LEWIS'S
LEWIS'S (Staffordshire) LTD.

NEXT WEEK

Evenings at 7-0
Matinees Thursday and Saturday—2-30

THE SADLER'S WELLS TRUST LTD.
(In Association with the Arts Council of Great Britain)

presents

Sadler's Wells Theatre Ballet
and FULL ORCHESTRA

Repertoire:

Le Lac Des Cygnes	:	Les Sylphides
Haunted Ballroom	:	Selina
The Gods Go A-Begging		
La Fete Etrange	:	Facade
Les Rendezvous	:	Capriol Suite
Divertissements		

WHY NOT HAVE A

OBTAINABLE AT THE THEATRE BARS . . .

JOULE'S
STONE ALE

Above. Extract of a theatre programme for 'As You Like It', playing the Theatre Royal week beginning 23rd May 1949. The following week's fateful engagement of the Sadler's Wells Theatre Ballet is advertised.

Flames were soon leaping 40ft into the air, and burning splinters threatening to ignite neighbouring properties in Piccadilly[115]. Cars in the neighbouring Motor Mart garage were hastily driven away out of danger and the surrounding roads were sealed off due to the number of hosepipes littering the streets.

Manager Percy Hughes was woken up by police who escorted him to the burning building, whilst still wearing his pyjamas beneath his overcoat. He watched the conflagration along with the owner Frederick Peake and John Abberley of the Evening Sentinel. It took three and a half hours to bring the fire under control using appliances from all the pottery towns and additional support from the Staffordshire brigade.

When it was safe to do so, Hughes entered the theatre through the Grand Circle staircase, still intact, to retrieve papers from the office, now deposited at Stoke-on-Trent City Archives. Although the cause of the fire was never determined, the previously mentioned rewiring work was taking place at the time in the void between ceiling and the roof, with the workmen using candlelight for illumination[116].

The visiting Sadler's Wells Ballet lost their costumes, sets and instruments, along with the dancers' personal possessions. Thanks to the donations of similar companies the ballet managed to reopen the following week in Hull. Waterlogged by the firefighting efforts, the company's unique music manuscripts were thought destroyed however they were later dried out and recovered[117].

Whilst still smouldering the site was surveyed by architect George Greaves who determined that although the auditorium and stage were destroyed, the exterior walls were intact and that reconstruction would be possible[118]. Frederick Peake thus announced that day, whilst sitting in his office at the theatre, his intention to rebuild the theatre as soon as possible[119]. Rebuilding was estimated as costing £150,000, with the building underinsured for only £30,000[120].

Demolition work began almost immediately to make the property safe. The stage house onto Brunswick Street was surrounded in scaffolding and the gable ends, roof beams and decorative cornice removed[121]. After demolition work, only the exterior walls of the theatre were left, including the wall facing Brunswick Street and the entrance block onto Pall Mall. Also demolished were buildings to the right of the Pall Mall entrance in order to allow machinery to enter the site.

Plans were rapidly drawn up for a modern theatre with seating for 1,800, a capacity large enough to attract the larger touring companies. Following the war, licences were required for new building projects. These were restricted exclusively for essential works such as new housing and industrial premises. Despite minister of works Charles Key being impressed by the low amount of steel in the design, the license application was declined[122]. Over 52,000 local persons signed a petition to get the decision overruled and finally in March 1950, following a change of government and cabinet, permission was granted to construct a new roof in order to preserve the remains[123]. Licenses for the internal work were to be granted at a later date.

Construction finally began on 10th April 1950 and proceeded quickly. Work was carried out by the firm of Cornes and Co., with Edward Forshaw and George Greaves the architects.

During excavation work for the proscenium arch foundations, the land opened up in several places, almost taking one of the workmen with it[124]. The theatre was built on an old footrill mine and the weight of the new steelwork and the excavations had caused the workings to reopen. There was a large hole beneath the stage area and another over 13ft across and 25ft deep beneath the location of the new balcony[125]. Work halted until a solution was devised, involving pumping liquid concrete under pressure into the workings to stabilise the site. This leaked into the local drains, requiring a team of men to clear them before it set. Work soon restarted.

The theatre was the first built in the country following the war[126]. 840 patrons could be seated in the stalls, 586 in the dress circle and 372 in the upper circle, 1,800 in total. The fronts of the balconies were adorned with quilt effect plaster, decorated in red and gold on a peach background. The carpets were in deep red and fawn, with matching auditorium seats and curtains. The upper balcony was incredibly steep, and so high that views of the front and rear of the stage were restricted. The side boxes offered similar restrictions[127].

The stage was smaller than before, 58ft wide and 33ft deep with a 40ft proscenium opening. Wing space was provided only on stage right with a scene dock 15ft wide. Sixty sets of counterbalanced gear were installed to allow scenery to be flown upwards into the flies, and over three hundred lighting points were provided on the stage, controlled by state of the art electronic console at the rear of the second circle with 96 dimmers.

A lift was provided down to the stage from the actors' numerous dressing rooms[128]. A five ton safety curtain was installed in case of fire, along with a battery operated emergency lighting system. The auditorium was air conditioned for comfort and licensed bars provided for patrons, along with a snack bar. The rebuilding was estimated to have cost £250,000[129].

Although the original Matcham entrance in Pall Mall was renovated and connected to the new auditorium, plans were developed for a spacious new entrance facing Marsh Street with a cafe above, however this was never constructed[130].

The night before opening, whilst work was frantically continuing around them, the Midland Home Service broadcast a live radio programme from the stage entitled "A Theatre Rebuilt – The Story of the Destruction and Reconstruction of the Theatre Royal Hanley". For twenty minutes at 7.30pm, BBC commentators James Pestridge and David Martin interviewed director Frederick Peake, manager Percy Hughes, lighting operator Marion Aldridge, architect George Greaves and others as to the story of the theatre's past and future[131]. That night the orchestra pit was accidentally flooded, damaging some of the handwritten music scores. It resulted in a frantic effort to pump out the water and make it ready for the opening[132].

Opening night came on Tuesday 14th August 1951 in the annual Wakes week. The Lord Mayor Horace Barks and his wife, the mayors of Newcastle, Stafford, Congleton and Colwyn Bay, Mr. and Mrs. Donald Wolfit, Mr. and Mrs. Emile Littler and the directors assembled on the stage as the Lord Lieutenant of the County H. Wallace-Copland cut the ribbons crossing the proscenium to formally declare the theatre open. After more speeches, a celebratory verse from Donald Wolfit and the presentation of bound programmes to those on stage, the national anthem was sung before the overture commenced and the new theatre's first night got underway[133].

The first production was Emile Littler's national tour of Irving Berlin's hit musical 'Annie Get Your Gun'. It starred Peggy Powell as Annie Oakley and Arthur Clarke as her love interest Frank Butler. Over seventy artistes were involved, with an augmented pit orchestra led by Arthur Logan. The show had only recently finished its 1,304 show run at the London Coliseum. Top price seats would have cost 10s. 6d. in the Grand Stalls, but just 4s. 6d. in the rear of the 2nd circle[134].

Old Theatres in the Potteries

Above. Flyer for the 1952 engagement at the Theatre Royal of Laurel and Hardy as part of the variety bill.

Old Theatres in the Potteries

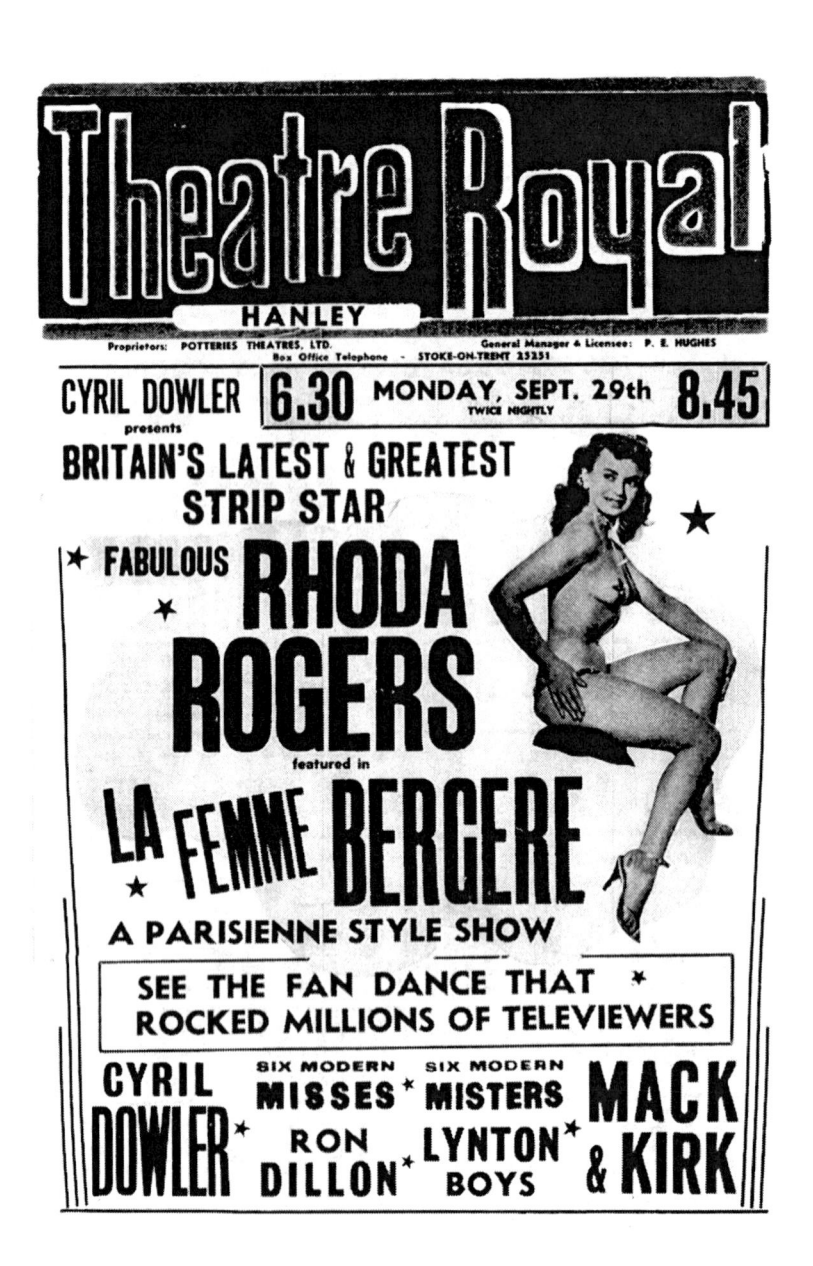

Above. Poster for the 1958 show 'La Femme Bergere', one of the titillation shows booked into the venue during its later years

In the first few months after reopening the people of Stoke-on-Trent could have sampled Billy Cotton and his Band in 'Wakey Wakey', Harry Lester and his Hayseeds, the play "The Cocktail Party" by T.S. Eliot, the musical comedy "The Belle of New York", or even the ice spectacle "Festival on Ice" In 1952, Stan Laurel and Oliver Hardy played a week-long engagement beginning 31st March as part of a variety bill[135].

It was not long before the audiences were dwindling due to the popularity of television. The theatre was losing money on a weekly basis and Percy Hughes was finding it hard to secure suitable acts. Potteries Theatres Ltd. called it a day in 1954 and the theatre was sold to Moss Empires, the major nationwide chain of variety theatres[136].

Problems continued with booking sufficient quality attractions, despite being part of the circuit and money continued to be lost. Manager Hughes felt "ashamed" that the venue was forced to present nudist shows. In 1958, year-round operations at the theatre ceases as Moss Empires reverted to the old practice of closing theatres over the summer in order to save money[137].

A solution seemed to present itself in 1961. A deal was struck whereby the theatre would be leased to the Mecca company in the afternoons to offer bingo sessions, whilst live theatre would continue in the evenings. The manager was told that their jobs would all be safe for many years to come and with that, he proceeded to his summer holiday in July 1961, the theatre being closed for its summer break at the time[138].

Whilst away, Moss Empires sold the theatre to Mecca and announced its closure with an almost immediate conversion to a bingo hall. Leslie McDonald, managing director of Moss Empires, said at the time:

> "Neither touring shows nor artists wanted to go there, and when we managed to get them to appear, the public would not support them. Intellectual theatregoers there (in Hanley) have written to express their views, saying that it is entirely the fault of the people of Hanley that the theatre has closed."[139]

The Stoke-on-Trent Amateur Operatic Society cancelled rehearsals of its production of 'The Most Happy Fella', booked into the venue for the following year[140]. This production would later be staged at the nearby Gaumont, the owners of which made the stage available for booking by the local amateur societies.

On Friday, October 20th 1961 the Mecca Bingo Club at the Theatre Royal, Hanley opened and television star Hughie Green was on hand to call the numbers for the first bingo game[141]. Five games would have cost a player just 2 shillings. Mecca did however announce that the theatre and stage would still be bookable by groups on select dates as the stage machinery was still in place. This took place throughout the early sixties with 'Flower Drum Song' (1962), 'Oklahoma!' (1963), 'The King and I' (1964) and 'The Pajama Game (1965) all presented by the local amateur societies.

A casino, the 'Top Hat Club', was opened on the stage in September 1966. Various games were provided for customers including roulette, blackjack, and baccarat, in an atmosphere of velvet curtains, red carpets, shaded lights and background music. A free buffet was served by waitresses for the patrons[142]. The club had previously agreed to make way for two weeks in 1967 to allow the use of the stage by the amateur societies, however it seemed obvious that this would prove an inconvenience to the operators.

Faced with losing the last large theatre in the city, the council commissioned a report from the City Architect regarding the suitability of converting an existing theatre into a multi-purpose 'civic theatre'. The verdict on the Theatre Royal was damning. As it stood the building didn't meet the key criteria set down by the Cultural Activities sub-committee. The visibility in the auditorium, especially in upper circle, was said to be poor as were the acoustics. The foyer and refreshment areas were also "completely inadequate". The stage was deemed too shallow compared to its width and the lack of wing space on stage left was cited as a major problem.

The architect's recommendations, if the scheme were approved, would have included the installation of an apron stage projecting into the auditorium to increase its versatility. The stalls would also have been remodelled with a stronger rake to improve sight lines, also having the effect of providing space for a larger refreshment room. The upper circle would be closed off and masked due to its sight problems. This would have remedied the problems in the auditorium, but the stage problems could not be reconciled due to the confines of the site. In the meeting of the sub-committee on the 13th December 1966 it was decided to make no further enquiries regarding the venue, and instead to investigate adapting Burslem's Queen's Hall[143].

At about the same time the North Staffs. Amateur Operatic and Dramatic Society attempted to bring forward their production of 'West Side Story' from October to April 1967. Mecca refused, and announced that the stage would not be available for future productions[144]. This production was moved to the Queen's Theatre in Burslem which was hastily adapted by the council for theatrical use. The Queen's, along with the Gaumont in Hanley, became the home of the local amateur operatic societies for many years to come whilst the Theatre Royal continued with its bingo and casino operations.

A Return to Live Theatre

In September 1981 Mecca announced that the bingo operation was to close[145], and the building was subsequently put up for sale for £210,000[146]. In response the 'Theatre Royal Trust' was formed by a group of local enthusiasts in order to raise the money needed to purchase the theatre. Meetings were held with the county council, Stoke-on-Trent City Council and Newcastle Borough Council in order to obtain funding, but this was not forthcoming[147].

After nine months of discussions, during which time the auditorium was flooded to a depth of 14ft by a burst pipe[148], the trust took a lease on the building from Mecca[149]. The rent would be charged at £30,000 annually for two years followed by an option to purchase for £200,000. They continued their fundraising efforts in order to purchase the theatre, as well as for the estimated £250,000 to repair, redecorate and relight the venue[150]. Both Ken Dodd and the Earl of Lichfield agreed to be patrons, and Second City Management were hired to help with the fundraising[151]. The pantomime 'Babes in the Wood' was booked for Christmas whilst a team of volunteers set about renovating and cleaning up the theatre. The circles were cleaned, having been unused for sixteen years, parts reseated and the building partially rewired. The bingo tables were still in place and stage equipment had to be hired in as the original equipment was removed during its years as a bingo hall[152].

After sixteen years dark, the Theatre Royal reopened on Monday 13th December 1982 with the pantomime 'Babes in the Wood'. In front of the 1,000 audience members, a small ceremony was performed by the former manager Percy Hughes. The opening almost didn't happen as the licence to operate was only delivered from the council three hours before the curtain rose[153]. The pantomime was a success, generating £10,000 profit which was spent on new amplifiers, microphones and speakers[154].

At the start of 1983, the theatre looked set to die an early death as management disagreements forced the staff of Second City Management to leave[155] and the police to be called in over a company set up by the two groups[156]. To top it off, band 'The Killjoys' cancelled their concert in January when sound and lighting equipment failed to materialise at the theatre[157].

By March 1983 things seemed to take a turn for the better when the trust became a charity, lead by Wolstanton solicitor Charles Deacon[158]. 'Full House' signs went up outside the theatre for the first time since the sixties when Bill Kenwright's touring production of 'Joseph and his Amazing Technicolor Dreamcoat' visited[159].

Finances were eventually secured from bankers Hill Samuel; with £200,000 securing the freehold and £100,000 for restoration work[160]. New stage equipment was installed, along with five chandeliers from Butlin's Clacton camp[161].

The theatre was staffed with a large number of volunteers, doing jobs ranging from selling programmes, ushers, cleaning and backstage work[162].

The Theatre Royal became a plc. in July 1984 with around £250,000 of capital raised from 12 local shareholders[163]. The Footlights club was also opened at the theatre, providing licensed premises open during the day for "meetings, parties, luncheons, dinners and any other functions."

The trust decided that the future lay in becoming a producing house, creating its own shows from scratch. They believed that it was one of the "few theatres technically capable of mounting as well as presenting" major productions[164].

The first was a co-production with the Kenneth More Theatre of 'The Rocky Horror Show' in May 1984[165], the success of which led Theatre Royal Plc. to tour the show almost continuously from September 1984 through to August 1988. The production actively encouraged audience participation, with patrons often turning up in fishnet stockings and basques, pelting the actors with rice, water and Kit Kats and shouting at the actors from the auditorium. The show was incredibly successful and closed only after creator Richard O'Brien removed the rights in order to mount his own production. He apparently had a dislike for the Theatre Royal production, calling it "vulgar"[166]. In 1987 the production helped the theatre to gain a cash surplus of £186,000[167].

1984 saw more in-house productions sent out to tour the country, including 'They're Playing Our Song', the hit Broadway and West End musical[168], and 'Once a Catholic' with Fenella Fielding. The pantomime for that year, 'Cinderella' with Lewis Collins and Clodagh Rogers, was also produced in-house.

Perhaps the biggest production to come out of the Theatre Royal was a revival of the Broadway musical 'Cabaret'. Starring Wayne Sleep as the emcee and directed by 'Cats' choreographer Gillian Lynne, the show toured the country for twelve weeks, appearing in Hanley in April 1986. It opened at the Strand Theatre in London the following month. Before closing in May 1987, the show hit the headlines when it became first musical in the West End to play without an orchestra. The pit musicians went on strike after Wayne Sleep flicked orange peel into the orchestra, leaving Toyah Wilcox and the rest of the cast to perform acapella[169].

The theatre acquired what very few possessed, a chapel. An old dressing room on the fourth floor was converted and Father John Pawson presided. The only other theatre in the country with an equivalent facility as the National Theatre, London[170].

The eighties also saw a large number of touring productions visiting the venue, featuring a plethora of eighties stars. These included Peter Adamson in 'A Taste of Honey'(1986), Patrick Mower in 'Gaslight' (1986), the UK tour of 'A Chorus Line' (1987), Anthony Quayle in 'Dandy Dick' (1988), Alvin Stardust in 'Godspell', 'Daisy Pulls it Off' (1987), 'The Importance of Being Hilda', an adaptation of Oscar Wilde's famous play starring Dame Hilda Bracket and Doctor Evadne Hinge (1988), and John Inman in 'Bedside Manners' (1989).

Things looked good for the theatre, but it was not to last for long. In June 1987 the trust was locked in a legal battle with former director Paul Barnard, who had been invited to resign the previous September[171]. Barnard was sued for £550,000 worth of takings for a Spanish tour of 'The Rocky Horror Show'. In a counterclaim, Barnard and Spanish producer Angela Taprogge sued Theatre Royal Hanley Plc. for upwards of £50,000 they loaned for the production of 'Cabaret'[172]. There was a very real threat of closure at the time as creditors had a petition to compulsorily wind up the theatre, which was later dismissed[173].

Bookings from the local amateur societies increased after 1989 when the nearby Odeon closed. It prompted letters to the *Evening Sentinel* complaining about the Royal's poor acoustics, steep gallery and small foyer[174].

The theatre's exterior was used as a filming location for the 1989 Carl Reiner film 'Bert Rigby You're A Fool' starring Robert Lindsay. It stood in for the Ritz Entertainment Centre in the title character's home town.

Money worries continued to plague the venue. Finally, the theatre was put up for sale in 1993 as a going concern. Theatre Royal Hanley (Management) Ltd. had built up £300,000 of debts, £15,000 of which were owed to a local advertising company who had obtained another winding up order, later postponed[175]. Another local action group, "The Potteries Theatre Royal Action Committee", was set up in order to raise £200,000 to buy the theatre in the event of the management being wound up[176].

The theatre stopped taking cash bookings and several planned shows were cancelled. The uncertainty at the time was so great that the electricity board began taking weekly meter readings to ensure payment[177]. Closure finally came to the venue in May 1993.

As if the events at the Theatre Royal was not enough, director Charles Deacon was declared bankrupt, being owed £200,000 by the theatre[178]. He was later found guilty of fraud in 1996 and sentenced to nine years in prison. Along with James Fuller, he took £11,250,000 from various companies and individuals in an "advance fee fraud", claiming he had the backing of the CIA[179].

The action trust, now renamed the "Potteries Theatre Royal Purchase and Restoration Trust", had their offer of £100,000 accepted for the building They applied to become a registered charity and aimed to reach their target with the sale of commemorative T-shirts and mugs[180]. The contents, fixtures and fittings of the theatre were auctioned off by the Sheriff of Staffordshire[181], and purchased by the trust in partnership with several local amateur operatic societies, at a cost of £9,300.

A new management company was formed, Potteries Theatre Royal (Management) Ltd, headed by Michael Fontaine[182]. Following the reinstatement of the entertainment license in September, the theatre reopened. The first show was the Stoke-on-Trent Amateur Operatic Society's production of 'The King and I' on 27th September 1993[183].

Another volunteer-based renovation scheme was started, this time with workers paid in 1938 monies[184]. It was soon revealed that chief executive Fontaine and artistic director Simon Ellingham were previously the heads of a collapsed London theatre company[185].

In an effort to obtain council funding, the management commissioned a report on the fabric of the building, stating that it would cost £658,579.89 to make the building safe[186]. This included around £350,000 of new electrical installations, a £200,000 fire sprinkler system, fire dampers, emergency lighting, a fire conductor, asbestos removal and a fresh drinking water supply. The report also claimed that repairs over the years had been made by "unqualified and unskilled workers". The report backfired as the council threatened to revoke the operating license due to the inherent danger in the building. They permitted the theatre to operate from an external generator until the results of a separate survey were known. This second survey downgraded the estimate to just £150,000[187].

More money worries hit the theatre when the TSB, owners of the building, demanded final payment be made on the loan. This couldn't be met and the trust was evicted. On Friday 24th June 1994 the twenty-two workers at the theatre were made redundant as with no premises to trade from, the management company went into voluntary liquidation[188]. The building was subsequently put on the market[189].

Debts had racked up to £139,750. Hundreds of creditors were listed at the insolvency hearing, including BBC Pebble Mill, the Performing Rights Society, Newcastle Amateur Operatic Society, the Inland Revenue, and those who had purchased advance tickets[190]. Curiously, several assets were found to be missing from the theatre including a grand piano, kitchen equipment, show memorabilia and furniture. The under-stage area was also found to be flooded with raw sewage[191].

Fontaine was disqualified as a company director for four years in 1997 as a result of his tenure at Hanley, due to him continuing to trade in the knowledge that bills couldn't be paid. Fellow director Brian Pridmore was also barred for three years[192]. Fontaine and Ellingham were later arrested in Spain over other collapsed businesses and imprisoned there for seven months[193].

Don Steward, a former member of the theatre's governing trust and market researcher, purchased the Theatre Royal in November 1994[194]. He was joined by investors Colin Fisher, Dennis Stephenson - chairman of the Tate gallery, and Peter York. Steward planned to fill the theatre with a mix of "pantomime, big touring shows, amateur productions and one off concerts".

Steward purchased the theatre in the knowledge that a study was being carried out into restoring the former Regent Cinema and Victoria Hall[195]. When published, it described the theatre as "unremarkable in its architecture, with cramped facilities". It went on to say:

> "There are serious limitations on the extent to which the Theatre Royal can be improved and it would be impossible to make sufficient improvement to enable it to host large scale modern touring musicals, opera and ballet of the highest quality."[196]

The first pantomime under Steward's tenure was 'Aladdin' starring Jack Wild, however poor ticket sales forced its early closure[197]. 40,000 visitors came in the first six months of his ownership, but the venue was still running at a loss. One big success was 'The Blues Brothers', filling the house during its two visits[198].

Not surprisingly given the theatre's previous track record this management team didn't last long and the doors were closed again on 23rd April 1996. Debts of up to £400,000 forced Don Steward and his fellow directors to put the company into liquidation. A last minute plea for a loan from the council was refused, having already loaned them £120,000, prompting the almost immediate closure of the theatre[199]. Producer Bill Kenwright was the largest creditor, owed £25,000, with others including lawyers Harbottle and Lewis, Customs and Excise and the Inland Revenue[200].

This news came just two weeks after the announcement that the Regent Cinema and Victoria Hall were to receive a £14,000,000 refurbishment as part of the new 'Cultural Quarter'.

The building was put up for sale with an asking price of just £50,000 and the entire theatre contents were auctioned off for a total of £11,360. The crest which hung above the proscenium was sold for £220 to local signage firm Weston Signs and the sound system went for £780[201]. Other lots included a pantomime rickshaw and a 6ft high pantomime postbox[202].

The theatre was locked up and deserted, presumably permanently.

In October 1996, *The Sentinel* announced that a mystery buyer had purchased the building. Rumour was rife until it was announced that it had been snapped up by local businessman Mike Lloyd, owner of a chain of local record shops[203]. Initially undecided as to his plans for the site, he considered such ideas as a theme restaurant, concert venue, or even using the land as a car park[204]. He chose, however, to use it as a theatre and concert venue, and renovation work was underway by July 1997[205].

The theatre was stripped previously, with pipes, wiring and contents removed[206]. This left a lot of work to be completed during the renovation.

A new roof was fitted, and the theatre was totally rewired, relit, and repainted. A new heating system was installed and new, larger dressing rooms created. The seats in the stalls were replaced with those of a removable kind, allowing use as a standing-only music venue. Over £1,000,000 was spent on the building and upon completion the venue was renamed, becoming 'The Royal'. An accompanying neon sign was installed on the repainted blue exterior on Pall Mall.

Ken Dodd opened the building on Sunday 29th November 1997 before an open day and a concert by group 'Cast'. One-night shows were planned to be the staple of the theatre; Lloyd said that he was not "looking for war" with the neighbouring Victoria Hall and Regent Theatre, soon to open.

The first pantomime in the new venue was 'Cinderella'. Directed by Jim Davidson it starred Ruth Madoc, Diane Louise Jordan, Mr Blobby, Johnny Casson, a young Stephen Mulhern and local actor Tim Churchill[207].

Other shows presented included single night runs of 'Michael Ball in Concert', 'The Solid Silver 60s Show', 'The Chuckle Brothers', 'Des O'Connor Live on Stage', 'Elvis Experience', and Elkie Brooks. Comedy shows were also staged from the likes of Ken Dodd, Alan Davies, and Roy 'Chubby' Brown. Some productions were presented over the whole week including the Porthill Players' production of 'South Pacific', Newcastle Amateur Operatic Society's 'Calamity Jane', 'Girl's Night Out' and 'Cinderella on Ice'.

The Regent Theatre reopened in 1999 giving The Royal competition. 1999's panto Aladdin, with The Grumbleweeds, battled The Regent's 'Cinderella' with an all-star cast including Cannon and Ball and Melinda Messenger.

Above. The Pall Mall facade in 2010, as part of the Liquid/Jumpin' Jaks complex.

The Royal did not have to compete with the newcomer for long as on 30th March 2000, Mike Lloyd's businesses collapsed with debts of £839,000[208]. It was reported at the time that the Royal was profitable and due to break even within two and a half years, as per the business plan[209]. KPMG were appointed as the liquidators, tasked with recovering as much of the debt as possible. The fixtures and fittings were auctioned off, and the building sold to Luminar Leisure. The internal space was gutted, and split into two venues, Jumpin' Jaks and Liquid nightclub.

Little of the original theatrical interior remains, however the upper circle and lighting suite are still present and have been the home to the local pigeon population in recent years. The Brunswick Street facade of 1871, and the Pall Mall facade of 1887 can still be seen from the street, the former partially adapted to become the entrance of the new venues.

Circus Music Hall, Hanley

In 1864, a wooden hippodrome and circus was constructed in Church Street, Hanley, advertised as "the largest and most beautiful building that ever was erected in the provinces."[210] It was occupied for three months by J. W. Myers' American Circus, opening on Saturday 18th June 1864. Myers had just completed an unsuccessful season at the Alhambra Circus, Manchester[211].

The opening night acts comprised of horse riding and rope dancing, along with trapeze and vaulter acts 40ft off the ground. The acts changed over the residency; during the closing few weeks, some of the acts were the "Walls of Troy"- a pyramid of men, "Jacob in Search of his Father", "The Dancing Irishman", and a grand equestrian spectacular[212]. Potteries people would have paid 6d to enter the gallery, 1s for the pit and promenade, and 2s 6d for a box. The proprietor offered a matinee performance to local schoolchildren on the 19th of September, during which the "Young Julien" fell 52ft from the trapeze and landed on his head, to the horror of the gathered crowd[213].

It was adapted the following year, reopening as the Victoria Music Hall[214] operated by Mr. J. Prince. Renamed the Prince of Wales Music Hall by 1866, it was home to Newsome's Cirque with a mix of circus acts and music hall acts presented in the arena[215].

Another name change to the Circus Music Hall had occurred by 1867[216]. The venue played host to public meetings as well as entertainments – a group of iron workers met there on 20th January 1868 to discuss their wage cut[217].

Whilst the theatre in Brunswick Street was rebuilt between 1870 and 1871, its former manager John Windley took over the circus and presented a successful month-long season beginning in Wakes week. He brought acts "somewhat above the ordinary Music Hall standard" to the theatre, with the description of the acts in trade paper *The Era* as follows[218]:

> "M. and Madam Loretto, who bring down great applause on their spade dances, acrobatic feats, doubling fiddling, and hat spinning. Mr. G.J. Ritz, attired as a North American Indian, plays with great skill as many as ten tambourines at once. Mr and Mrs

Old Theatres in the Potteries

Barney Roberts appear in an entertainment called 'Ireland in Shade and Sunshine'; and Messrs Bradley and Bathurst give appreciable specimens of the good old Richardsonian style of drama. The great attraction this week has been the Brothers Wainratta, whose performances on the tight and slack wire have been deservedly applauded to the echo. Each evening's programme has wound up with the ballet 'Three Lovers Too Many' by the Misses Wilbraham and Green' Mr W. Laffar and others. The band is efficient, and Mr. E. B. Henry is a good chairman"

During this period of dominance over the town's entertainments, the building went through yet more name changes. These included the Royal Pottery Music Hall (taking its name from the Brunswick Street theatre), Royal Circus Music Hall[219], and Theatre Royal[220]. The music hall acts were dropped for drama, and with the engagements of tragedian James Holloway and the return of John Windley the building was retitled the 'Theatre Royal, Grand Opera House and Temple of Varieties'. This brief flirtation with legitimate theatre did not last however and it reverted back to the Circus Music Hall following the reopening of the Theatre Royal in March 1871[221]. It was said to be a "second-class Music hall where liquors were sold" and in 1871, a production of 'The Battle of Trafalgar' was staged. This contained gunfire and explosions and culminated with the death of Nelson, seemingly standard fare for the venue at that time[222].

Following a takeover by Thomas Rogers, a stage license was applied for and refused with the residents of the area and lessee of the Theatre Royal opposing[223]. The building was subsequently renamed the 'People's Music Hall and Circus' after Rogers went into business with Mr. J. Warrilow.

Rogers soon announced his intention to replace the wooden circus with a permanent brick building. Work progressed quickly, and the venue closed on Saturday 19th July 1873 with the business transferring to the new building adjacent to the south, again called the People's Music Hall. Demolition began on the old site just two days after closing.

Development of the People's Music Hall / Imperial Circus

Above. 1865 Ordnance Survey Map. Shows the wooden circus building on Church Street then known as the Victoria Music Hall.

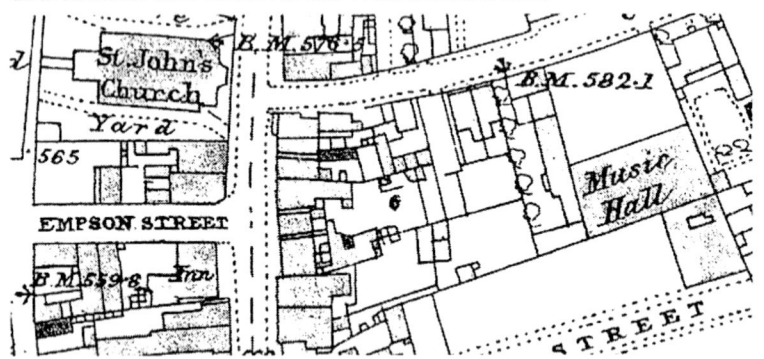

Above. 1879 OS Map showing the 2nd People's Music Hall, constructed of brick in 1873 to replace the wooden circus.

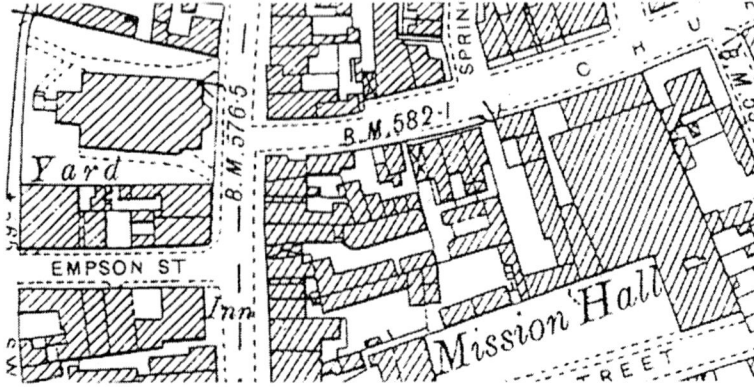

Above. 1898 OS Map, showing the Imperial Mission Hall, formerly Circus, extending to Church Street and to Glass Street.

People's Music Hall, Hanley

The new People's Music Hall, Glass Street, was erected by Thomas Rogers at "considerable expense" in 1873[224], just south of the building up to that point called the People's Music Hall. Designed by owner Thomas Rogers, the music hall was in the "theatre shape" as opposed to an arena like the previous venue. The hall was of a large size, said to be second only to the Alhambra in London, with a plain but large brick exterior. It could hold 4,000 audience members over pit, gallery, and side, centre and stage boxes. At the time of opening, the internal decoration was not complete, owing to the speed of the building's erection[225].

The stage measured 36ft wide and 26ft deep, with the proscenium opening being 37ft tall. Skylights in the ceiling allowed sunlight to illuminate the auditorium, supplemented by gaslight throughout. The total cost of the new music hall, for both site and construction, was said to be over £9,000. Prior to opening the Borough Surveyor was taken on a tour of the new site and made several recommendations as for the safety of the audience. The entrance to the new building faced onto Glass Street, a new street at that time. At opening, the hall was run by Thomas Rogers and J. Warrilow.

Opening night was on Monday 21st July 1873, just two days after the closure of the previous 'People's Music Hall' next door. Guests included Edward F. Bodley, mayor of Hanley, Colonel Roden M.P., George Melly M.P., and magistrates of the borough of Hanley.

Acts on stage that night included Mlle. Victoria and Signor Serano – Spanish gymnasts, Marie Courtenay - the operatic vocalist, Monsieur Grovini – pantomime acrobat and contortionist, Mr. and Mrs. Will Merchant with their sawmill act, selections from the band, a skipping rope dancer, Mr and Mrs Watson - comic burlesque artists, Leo Parni – a female impersonator, Mlle. Leonora – serio-comic vocalist, Lambert and Martin – "negro comedians", Polly Hanks - singer and dancer, Harry Linn – the comic vocalist and eccentric dancer, and a grand ballet with thirty artistes - a very full line-up! So full in fact that the only criticism given to the hall by the mayor was that "too much was given for the money, by which means the hall was kept open later than he should like it."

People's Music Hall

GLASS STREET, HANLEY.

GRAND CLASSICAL & POPULAR INSTRUMENTAL & VOCAL

CONCERT

ON TUESDAY, MARCH 27, 1877,

BY THE BAND OF HER MAJESTY'S

Coldstream Guards

CONDUCTOR: MR. FRED GODFREY;

WITH THE EMINENT BASSO,

SIGNOR FOLI.

PRICES OF ADMISSION:—

Private Boxes £1 11s. 6d.; Private Box Chairs (numbered & reserved), 6s. each.; Centre Chairs (numbered & reserved), 5s.; Side Centre Chairs (numbered and reserved), 3s. 6d.; Side Balconies and Promenade, 2s.; Pit, 1s.; Gallery, 6d.

TICKETS may be obtained at Messrs. ALLBUT and DANIEL'S, where a Plan of the Hall may be seen and places secured.

DOORS OPEN AT 7; COMMENCE AT 7 30.

Trains leave Hanley for all the Pottery Towns at close of Concert. SEE TIME BILLS.

ALLBUT AND DANIEL, PERCY STREET WORKS, HANLEY.

He did however praise the fact that the hall did not serve alcohol. Tickets for the night's entertainments cost 8d for a box, 6d in the promenade, 4d in the pit, and 3d in the gallery, and the proceeds for the night were donated to the North Staffordshire Infirmary, a grand total of £23 10s[226].

Some other music hall acts appearing during that first year included Verreyra - the man flute, Livingston and Nish - american boot and skate dancers and the Sisters Graham - sentimental vocalists[227].

During this period, certain acts were presented that would be unacceptable in the present day. "Negro Minstrel" acts were very popular, included "the talented trio" of "Mr J. L. Dixon, Miss Emily Mellon and Sambo Sutton"[228]. Many other acts of the same nature were touring around the country at the time, being a frequent part of the music hall line up, but especially popular at the People's Music Hall.

In 1877 Rogers was fined £90 for presenting stage acts without a licence; he had presented the pantomime 'Robinson Crusoe' for a time. At the hearing he complained that the forthcoming Batty's Circus would be offering similar entertainments without a licence, before finally conceding defeat[229].

Previous Page. Front cover of programme for a concert at the People's Music Hall, 27th March 1877.

Imperial Circus, Hanley

At the start of 1878, Thomas Rogers announced his intention to convert the 'People's Music Hall' into a hippodrome and circus[230]. The hall closed on 9th March for rebuilding, which involved extending the existing building towards Church Street over the site of the original wooden circus building[231]. When completed "the imposing edifice" was the largest building of its sort in the whole Potteries[232], measuring 120ft by 90ft and 40ft high[233]. 5,500 people could be housed in tiers of seats surrounding the central ring, split into pit, promenade, gallery and dress circle. The auditorium was lit with over 1,000 gaslights, with a system of ventilation employed to keep the temperature bearable. A number of dressing rooms and stores were built for the acts, along with a hayloft and stables for sixty horses located beneath the seating area. An entrance building was constructed facing Glass Street, housing a pay booth, cloakrooms and an entrance to the stables[234]. The architect was E. T. Harrison and internal decoration was by Matthew Hughes of Birmingham.

The new 'Imperial Circus' opened on Monday 16th September 1878 with an extended engagement of Charles Hengler's Circus. Not all the seats were sold that night, although Hengler's acts were said to be of a "good calibre". These included the Brothers Honrey – grotesque and comical hat manipulators, James Lloyd – daring hurdle act rider, James Henry Jr. - equestrian and somersault thrower, Amy Samwell – the celebrated equilibrist, and the "Lancers' Quadrilles on Horseback". The band was led by James Hare. Entrance to the stalls cost 3s, 2s for a box seat, 1s in the pit and promenade, and just 6d in the gallery. This was accessed from an entrance on Church Street whilst the other entrances remained on Glass Street. Strangely for the time, smoking was prohibited throughout the building[235].

The *Staffordshire Sentinel* saw another use for the building:

> "It will now be possible for the denizens of the Potteries to assemble literally "in their thousands", either to do honor to a popular man, to "demonstrate" on a local or national question, or to listen to a monstre choir"

Old Theatres in the Potteries

The arrival of the circus upset one of the neighbours, an architect living at 26 Church Street called William J. Palmer, who began legal action. This was halted by the unrelated departure of Mr. Hengler. Christmas 1878 saw the presentation of a series of oratorios, before Samuel Hague presented his travelling circus for 12 nights starting 10th March 1879. This further enraged Palmer who commenced further legal action, citing the noise of brass bands, banging of drums, singing and guns as disturbing to his family. The Hanley court passed an injunction against Hague, preventing him from causing a nuisance to the plaintiff[236].

As envisioned by the *Staffordshire Sentinel* at opening, the Imperial Circus held public meetings due to its large size. In 1880, the Mayor of Hanley, Mr. Bromley, presided over a meeting of Liberals. Mr. H. Broadhurst MP was present, as was Lord Granville, both of whom gave speeches[237]. Granville later returned in 1887[238].

A special service for the victims of the Fair Lady Pit disaster was held on 1st February 1880, with a collection for the wives and orphans of the victims raising over £27[239]. In 1883 2,000 coal miners whose wages had been cut by 10% due to the drop in the ironstone trade met at the circus to discuss their options[240].

The Imperial Cirque was taken over by Mark Dow, a "gentleman of great experience in the equestrian world" in 1881[241], reopening on 19^h March[242]. The programme including "the famed Sheldon family" - a family of equestrians, the vampires Thomas and James, along with

> "Beautiful Horses, Artistic Riders, Charming Lady Artists, Well bred Animals, Astounding Acrobats and Comical Clowns".

In the following month the Hanley and Shelton Philharmonic Society closed the season with a performance of 'Elijah'. Later that year the venue became the 'People's Varieties', opening on the 6th June managed by the Signor H. Balleni, "The Australian Blondin, Champion of Niagara Falls".

By August 1882 the Imperial Circus was being used by Rodney "Gipsy" Smith for his services, with the building eventually retitled the 'Imperial Mission Hall' as a result. Smith had set up in the circus following his dismissal from the Salvation Army[243], based at Batty's Circus in Tontine Street, after accepting a gift of a gold watch from the public. He was joined at the Imperial by his sister Miss. Smith, "the gypsy lass".

77

A disaster occurred at the building on Sunday, 22nd October 1882. Three hundred people were gathered in a prayer room during a "holiness" meeting when the floor gave way, plunging most of them into the circus stables below. Panic spread into the main hall where another event was taking place, leading to a dash for the exits. Further panic ensued when the gaslight was inadvertently extinguished, plunging them into darkness. Initial reports spoke of a horrendous disaster with many fatalities, including several trampled to death in the ensuing stampede. These proved to be false however, with only 43 injured - 5 men and 38 women. The cause of the incident was said to be due to the failure of a nine inch beam holding the floor supports[244].

The Imperial Mission Hall was used as a place of worship by the Hanley Mission Society throughout the 1890s[245], vacating the premises by 1903[246]. In the same year the Salvation Army opened a citadel on Glass Street adjacent to the building, on the site of what was the entrance to the circus. Following this, the entrance to the hall was located at the end of an alleyway between the Central Board School and the citadel in Glass Street.

The skating craze of the early 20th century resulted in the building becoming the Imperial Skating Rink in 1908. Shoe rental was 6d with free admission in the mornings, and visitors would skate around the area whilst the house band played[247].

The popularity of skating soon dwindled and conversion to a cinema followed, with the Imperial reopening on Thursday 29th August 1912. By this time, the interior had been reconfigured into a more conventional stall and balcony layout[248]. Always a silent picture house, the Imperial closed in December 1930. It reopened equipped with sound as 'The New Roxy' on 12th October 1931, the opening performed by film star Dodo Watts[249]. The cinema was relatively successful until the introduction of television caused audiences to dwindle. The Roxy closed on 3rd December 1961.

A later life saw the building becoming 'Mr. Smith's Nightclub', attracting top stars such as Cilla Black and Dusty Springfield[250]. The building was gutted by a fire in 1977, destroyed the building which was subsequently demolished. The site is currently home to 'Academy of Sound', a music equipment store, whilst the Salvation Army citadel still stands on Glass Street, disused.

Above. A current view of the site of the Imperial Circus, Glass Street. The circus ran along the rear wall of the Salvation Army.

Above. 1879 map of Hanley town centre. The Royal Alexandra Music Hall, later the Gaiety, can be seen just right of centre in New Street joined to the neighbouring New Inn.

Gaiety Theatre of Varieties, Hanley

The New Inn stood in New Street, now Goodson Street, Hanley.

In 1873 the New Inn opened a new addition to the premises, a music hall. Many of the larger public houses at the time were opening such premises. The drop cloth showed a depiction of Trentham Hall and the proprietor at opening was George Ashford. A name change followed to the Royal Alexandra Music Hall[251]. This was advertised as holding 500 persons over the pit and a gallery with a "good" bar; the hall was connected internally to the neighbouring New Inn. Entry to the pit would cost 3d, and the gallery 4d[252].

Leotard Bosco, real name James Frederick Greethead, took over the lease in 1884 and set about a scheme of refurbishment. The hall was completely redecorated including the addition of "coloured globes from the east." Mirrors were placed around the hall and the centre and side balconies were "cushioned" in leather. Attached to the theatre was a gentleman's lounge, similarly furnished. The boxes and pit were also renovated. The new drop cloth depicted a view of Mogador, and the works in the hall and adjoining inn were reported as costing £700.

It reopened on Monday 22nd December 1884 as the 'Gaiety Theatre of Varieties' with a programme comprising of Jenny Renforth – singer, W.M. Hicks and his "soldier dog", Monsieur Victor – gymnast and Miss. Massey the serio-comic. Before the festivities commenced Bosco appeared on the stage to announce that he aimed "to make the place such that any man could take his wife and not be ashamed of it."[253]

With the closure of the Theatre Royal for refurbishment in 1887, Bosco advertised heavily in the trade press for "the best acts", taking advantage of its near-monopoly of entertainment in the town for the duration of the construction work[254].

The building was demolished in the early 1890s to make way for the new 'Empire Theatre'.

Batty's Circus, Hanley

Batty's Circus was a touring circus that existed from the 1840s, if not earlier. When visiting Hanley, they previously set up in the yard at the back of the Swan Inn[255]. They presented acts such as the Fairy Ponies "the smallest in Europe", The Antipodean Wonder and the "Military Entree". A wooden building was eventually constructed to house the circus in around 1878 on land off Tontine Street. It was used by several circus groups over the years; Harmston's Circus was resident during 1880[256], as was Boswell's Circus in 1886[257].

'General' Booth of the Salvation Army took a three year lease on the circus in November 1882 at the same time that he purchased the theatre in Tunstall, using the venue for his religious meetings in the town[258].

Gypsy Smith preached at the circus before his "sacking" from the army, following which he set up at the Imperial Circus, Hanley. In 1885, the venue held faith-healing events run by Major Pearson of the Salvation Army. During these events thousands turned up to pray, with several apparently regaining the use of their limbs as a result. They were said to make use of "ejaculations expressive of their astonishment"[259].

Like the nearby Imperial Circus, the venue was utilised as a meeting venue. The Right Honourable J. Chamberlain M.P. addressed a large meeting at the circus in October 1884, in connection with the assembling of the National Liberal Federation. The venue was used to handle the overspill from the already-full Imperial Circus[260].

By 1886 James H. Elphinstone of the Theatre Royal had taken over the circus and embarked on a series of renovations. The interior was lined, boarded and decorated, with the fauteuil seats upholstered in crimson velvet. The total capacity was said to be 4,000. It reopened on Monday 7th March 1887 and was said to be "cosy and imposing"[261]. W. Batty Harmston was engaged as the equestrian director along with equestrian acts Nellie Bailey, Peppino G. Harmston and "Young Gill". Comedy on opening night was provided by Dan Philips, D'Altroy and "Flexmore". Elphinstone also ran similar circuses on the Isle of Man and in Hull[262].

The following month on 20th April 1887 the circus held a "Grand Jubilee Performance for the benefit of the Borough of Hanley Jubilee Funds"[263].

Along with the circus acts, boxing was often presented. In February 1893 such a match between W. Howe of Stoke and W. Jones of Hanley was halted by police, as in the words of the chief constable, it had gone "beyond the lines of fair and legitimate boxing".

The brothers Elphinstone had disposed of the venue by 1896 in preparation for the opening of their new Grand Theatre of Varieties and Circus, and the building was later demolished, making way for the new Post Office.

Old Theatres in the Potteries

Victoria Hall, Hanley

The Victoria Hall, Hanley was constructed on the former bowling green of the Queen's Hotel, purchased by the Hanley corporation as a new town hall. Designed by borough surveyor Joseph Lobley, the foundation stone was laid in August 1887 and the venue was opened on 4th October 1888[264]. The organ in the hall was built by the firm of Conacher for the Saltaire Exhibition of 1887 and was purchased by local manufacturer George Meakin, donating it to the new hall[265].

2,800 patrons could be seated over the ground floor and the two horseshoe-shaped galleries. Elgar's 'King Olaf' premiered at the hall and over the years the biggest names in all genres of music have played and conducted here. These have included Adelina Patti, Paul Robeson, the Halle Orchestra, John Barbirolli, Malcolm Sargent, Edward Elgar, Nat King Cole, Judas Priest - the list goes on[266]. The building was also a venue for sporting events, with boxing and wrestling being popular.

The mid 1990s saw a renovation programme as part of the new cultural quarter scheme along with the nearby Regent Theatre. An extension designed by Levitt Bernstein Associates was constructed to improve front-of-house facilities, featuring a four-storey atrium. The new extension also houses the Tourist Information Centre for the area and office space for the Ambassador Theatre Group, mangers of the venue[267]. Backstage facilities were also improved at the same time, extending into the retiring rooms of the neighbouring former courtrooms.

The hall reopened on Sunday 8th November 1998 with a gala concert featuring the City of London Sinfonia and the Ceramic City Choir[268].

Above. The exterior of the 1998 extension, designed by Levitt Bernstein Associates. It houses front-of-house facilities for the hall, office space and the Tourist Information Centre.

Old Theatres in the Potteries

BOROUGH OF HANLEY.

Opening of the Victoria Hall & Organ,

TOWN HALL, HANLEY.

FRIDAY, OCTOBER 5th,
GRAND ORGAN RECITAL
By A. L. PEACE, Esq, Mus. Doc.
Organist of the St. Andrew's Halls and Cathedral, Glasgow.

ADMISSION :—Balcony, **2s. 6d.**   Arena, **1s.**   Gallery, **6d.**

SATURDAY, OCTOBER 6th,
PEOPLE'S POPULAR NIGHT,
GRAND ORGAN RECITAL BY
J. KENDRICK PYNE, ESQ.,
Organist of the Town Hall and Cathedral, Manchester.

ADMISSION :—Balcony, **6d.**   Arena, **4d.**   Gallery, **2d.**

Doors open at 7 30.   Recitals commence at Eight o'clock.

TICKETS obtainable up to FIVE o'clock on the day of Recital at Messrs. ALLBUT & DANIEL, ATKINSON BROS., TIMMIS, and JAMES BEBBINGTON.

FRIDAY, OCTOBER 5th,

8 P.M.

ORGAN RECITAL

— BY —

A. L. Peace, Esq., Mus. Doc.

PROGRAMME.

I. Overture to the "Occasional Oratorio" .... *Handel.*

II. (*a.*) Air with Variations (G Major) .... *Haydn.*

    (*b.*) March (C Major) .... *Mozart.*

III. Prelude and Fugue (D Major) .... *J. S. Bach.*

IV. Offertorio (D Major) .... *Giovanni Morandi.*

V. Selection from the Opera "Faust" .... *Gounod.*
    (*a.*) Kermesse Coro—"'Sù, da bere."
    (*b.*) Romanza—"Quando a te lieta."
    (*c.*) Coro del Soldati—"Oh, gloria cinta d'allor."

VI. Grand Dramatic Fantasia "A Concert on the Lake" .... *Neukomm.*

VII. (1.) Theme from the Opera "Sylvana" .... *Weber.*
    (2.) Rondo (E Flat Major) ....

VIII. Overture .... "William Tell" .... *Rossini.*

DESCRIPTION OF THE ORGAN.

GREAT ORGAN.

1 Double Open Diapason ..metal.. 16 feet 61 pipes
2 Open Diapason .. ..metal.. 8 ,, 61 ,,
3 Gamba .. .. ..metal.. 8 ,, 61 ,,
4 Höhl Flöte .. ..wood.. 8 ,, 61 ,,
5 Harmonic Flute ..metal.. 4 ,, 61 ,,
6 Principal .. ..metal.. 4 ,, 61 ,,
7 Fifteenth ... .metal.. 2 ,, 61 ,,
8 Mixture, 3 ranks .. ..metal.. 183
9 Trumpet ...spotted metal.. 8 ,, 61 ,,

SWELL ORGAN.

10 Lieblich Bourdon .. ..wood 16 feet 61 pipes
11 Open Diapason .. ..metal 8 ,, 61 ,,
12 Stopped Diapason wood & metal 8 ,, 61 ,,
13 Voix Angelica .. wood & metal 8 ,, 61 ,,
14 Voix Celéstes .. spotted metal 8 ,, 49 ,,
15 Rohr Flöte .. .. ..metal 4 ,, 61 ,,
16 Principal .. .. ..metal 4 ,, 61 ,,
17 Piccolo .. .. ..metal 2 ,, 61 ,,
18 Mixture, 3 ranks .. ..metal 183
19 Contra Fagotto .. spotted metal 16 ,, 61 ,,
20 Cornopean .. spotted metal 8 ,, 61 ,,
21 Oboe .. .. spotted metal 8 ,, 61 ,,
22 Clarion .. .. spotted metal 4 ,, 61 ,,

CHOIR ORGAN.

23 Violin Diapason .. ..metal.. 8 feet 61 pipes
24 Dulciana .. .. ..metal.. 8 ,, 61 ,,
25 Clarabella .. ..wood .. 8 ,, 61 ,,
26 Lieblich Flute ..wood .. 4 ,, 61 ,,
27 Clarionet .. spotted metal.. 8 ,, 61 ,,

SOLO ORGAN.

28 Harmonic Flute .. ..metal.. 8 feet 61 pipes
29 String Gamba .. pure tin.. 8 ,, 61 ,,
30 Orchestral Oboe spotted metal 8 ,, 61 ,,
31 Vox Humana .. spotted metal 8 ,, 61 ,,
32 Tuba .. .. spotted metal 8 ,, 61 ,,

PEDAL ORGAN, CCC TO F, 30 NOTES.

33 Open Diapason .. ..wood.. 16 feet 30 pipes
34 Bourdon .. .. ..wood ..16 ,, 30 ,,
35 Quint .. .. ..wood ..10⅔ ,, 30 ,,
36 Violoncello .. ..metal.. 8 ,, 30 ,,
37 Trombone spotted metal & wood 16 ,, 30 ,,

ACCESSORIES.

38 Swell to Great.   42 Great to Pedals
39 Swell to Choir.   43 Choir to Pedals.
40 Solo to Great.   44 Solo to Pedals.
41 Swell to Pedals.
45 Tremulant to Solo by Pneumatic Piston and Draw Stop Action.

Four Composition Pedals to Great Organ.
Four Composition Pedals to Swell Organ.
Two Composition Pedals to Solo Organ
Pneumatic action to Great Organ and its Couplers.
Tubular Pneumatic action to Pedals.
Pneumatic double-acting Piston for controlling Great to Pedals Coupler.
The DRAW STOP JAMBS are Diagonal, at an angle of 45 degrees.
The DESK and FITTINGS are of Polished Walnut.
The DRAW STOP KNOBS are of Solid Ivory.
The Shutters of the Swell and Solo Boxes are perpendicular, and are controlled by balanced Pedals, so that the Shutters may remain open at any point ; the two Pedals for controlling these Organs are placed side by side, so that they may be worked simultaneously with one foot if needed.
The MANUALS are overhanging, and so arranged as to enable the Organist to play on two rows of keys with one hand at the same time.
The PEDAL BOARD is according to the Scale adopted by the College of Organists.
The TWO SWELL PEDALS also in the position adopted by the College of Organists.
The ORGAN is provided with four Reservoirs to supply wind at various pressures as required.
The BELLOWS are worked by steam power, with hand Auxiliary.

SUMMARY OF STOPS.

GREAT ORGAN .. .. 9 Stops .. .. 671 Pipes.   PEDAL ORGAN .. .. Stops .. .. 150 Pipes.
SWELL ORGAN .. .. 13 Stops .. .. 903 Pipes.   ACCESSORIES .. .. 8 Stops .. ..
CHOIR ORGAN .. .. 5 Stops .. .. 305 Pipes.
SOLO ORGAN .. .. 5 Stops .. .. 305 Pipes.   Grand Total 45 Stops   2334 Pipes.

MESSRS. PETER CONACHER & CO., HUDDERSFIELD, ARE THE BUILDERS AND VENDORS OF THE ORGAN.

Allbut and Daniel, Percy Street Printing Works, Hanley.

Old Theatres in the Potteries

Above. Illustration of the Empire Theatre, Hanley.

Empire Theatre, Hanley

The Empire Theatre was located on New Street (now Goodson Street), constructed on the site of the former Gaiety Theatre of Varieties.

The building was commissioned by the Provincial Music Hall Company, with plans from architect Frank Matcham who was given "carte blanche" to create "one of the best variety theatres that could be erected".

The facade faced onto New Street and was in the Italian style[269], with an iron and stained glass marquee over the entrance. The entrance hall, entered through polished wood doors, possessed a raised ornamental ceiling and was floored with encaustic tiles. From here a stone stairway led to a promenade running the width of the building, decorated with Japanese papers and mirrors. The auditorium itself could hold 1,500 over three levels, the stalls - split into pit and fauteuils, the balcony and the gallery. Private boxes were also in place[270]. All seats were said to have a clear view of the stage, and saloon bars were provided throughout for patrons.

Aesthetically, the balconies and proscenium arch had decoration of fibrous plaster in the Indian style, coated in gold and colour. A border of red marble framed the stage, and the arabesque backcloth was painted by Mr. Ryan. The ceiling housed a large dome and the auditorium was lit with the new electric light, powered by its own generator. Backstage seven dressing rooms were provided for the acts. The stage was built on piers over a pool of water used by neighbouring potteries, the stage floor being of concrete and boards.

The opening was not without controversy. Advertisements in the *Staffordshire Sentinel* proclaimed that the building would open under the patronage and presence of the mayors of Hanley, Stoke-upon-Trent and Newcastle. This caused great offence to certain members of the community, venting their anger with letters to the *Staffordshire Sentinel.*

They believed such an affiliation would "not promise to be a very desirable addition to our town and for the moral training of our young men and women", and that "the sexes would be brought together under conditions, and with results to be highly deplored."

Perhaps these letters had some effect for come opening night, Mr. Huntbach, mayor of Hanley, and Mr. Kirkham, mayor of Stoke, sent telegrams apologising for their absences, which were read out by manager Fred Gale. The opening performances on Monday 14th March 1893 were "heartfully enjoyed" by the audience, who were presented with such delights as Howlett's marionette theatre, Sam Jesson's character sketches, and the horizontal bar performances of 'The Voltynes'[271].

On 2nd November 1896, the Empire held the premier of motion pictures in the Potteries when William Paul's Theatregraph was presented as part of the variety bill[272].

In the late 1890s the building became part of the 'Leeds and Hanley Theatres of Varieties' company, formed in 1897 to take over and refurbish the Empire and the Princess Palace of Varieties in Leeds. The Consolidated Exploration and Finance Company, a front for Mr. Harrison Ainsworth, surreptitiously acted as an intermediate to purchase the theatres for £24,000, most of which on a mortgage, before selling them to Leeds and Hanley Theatres at an inflated price. Consolidated Exploration were also behind the Leeds and Hanley Theatre of Varieties company, both of which were subsequently put into liquidation. Ainsworth ended up with a handsome profit whilst the shareholders lost out financially[273]. Court cases against the company continued well into 1903 with several shareholders attempting to regain their investment. The judge at one such hearing deemed the company as being "scandalous and fraudulent from the beginning"[274].

The Empire was forced to close early in 1899 due to the collapse of the company, with the liquidators attempting to auction the building on 28th March 1899 however the bidding failed to reach the expected amount[275].

The theatre was later acquired by the Hanley Theatres and Circus company and partially rebuilt with improved stage facilities, becoming the 'King's Palace Theatre'. The theatre would now be a venue for drama, replacing the previous variety bill. The reopening was on Easter Monday 8th April 1901 with a piece called 'Fair Play' presented by the Milton Ray company[276]. In Act 3, a "spectacular scenic effect" was carried out depicting a landslide onstage[277].

The King's was leased to several groups in subsequent years including J.P Moore and B. Kennedy, and Edison and Barnum's Electric Picture Company[278]. By 1911, pictures had taken the whole bill - the week of 2nd January presented the pictures 'Dash to Death', 'The Tom-Tom Players',

'Blue Beard', and the "very exciting" 'The President's Special', linked with vaudeville from local singer Mabel Kingston[279].

Any success was short-lived as by the early twenties the building was empty. It was auctioned off at the North Stafford Hotel on the 4th June 1924 by the liquidators of Hanley Theatres Ltd, formerly Hanley Theatres and Circus, following the retirement of Charles Elphinstone[280].

Purchased by James Grant, a new main entrance was constructed adjacent to the Matcham frontage opening onto New Street at an angle. It opened as the 'Capitol' cinema in March 1925, seating 1,258 patrons and with a small stage 18ft deep. Becoming part of the ABC circuit in 1929 it remained as a venue for motion pictures until 24th August 1963 when the chain moved its operations to the new ABC Cine-bowl complex in Broad Street, Hanley. The Matcham facade had already been removed some years before hand[281].

After closure as a cinema it operated for a time as the Alpha Bingo Club before demolition in December 1965. After a period as a car park, a new building was constructed on the site in the mid seventies housing a Co-op department store, offices, and multi-story car park for the neighbouring Marks and Spencer.

Below. Goodson House in Goodson Street, Hanley, constructed on the site of the Empire Theatre.

Old Theatres in the Potteries

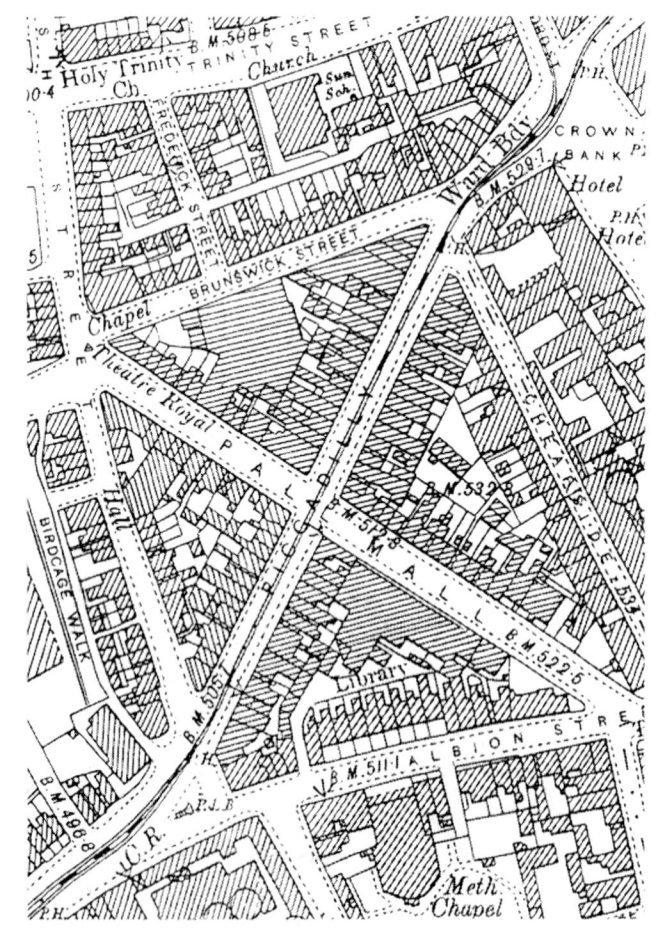

Above. 1898 Ordnance Survey map of Hanley town centre. The Lyric Hall can be seen just left of centre in between Marsh Street and Pall Mall.

Lyric Hall, Hanley

The Lyric Hall, Hanley was located in Pall Mall, opposite the entrance of the Theatre Royal. It was listed in *Kelly's Directory of Staffordshire* of 1912 as a theatre, located at 18 Marsh Street and operated by Samuel Brooks. The building was previously titled both the 'Central Lyric Hall' and 'Central Hall'[282]. It could seat 800 and possessed a 35ft by 13ft stage; the whole building being 40ft by 90ft[283]. In November 1897 Edison's Scenograph was exhibited in the hall with its "new living pictures"[284]. In a later life it became the Majestic Ballroom, which burned down in May 1964[285].

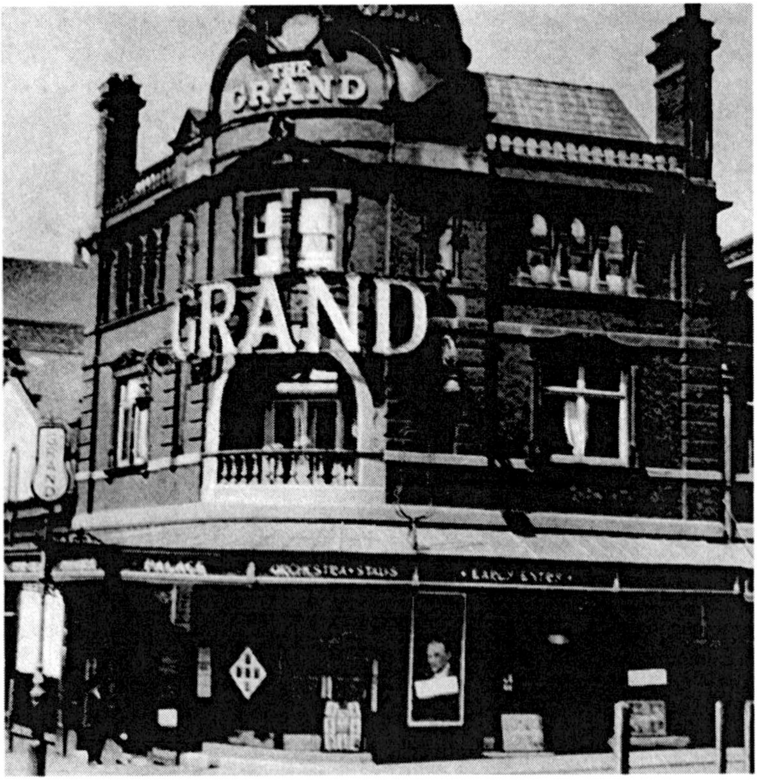
THE GRAND
GRAND
ORCHESTRA STALLS

Grand Theatre of Varieties, Hanley

Following their father's death, brothers Charles and George Elphinstone acquired his Hanley Theatres and Circus company and set about a scheme of expansion. This included the renovation of the Theatre Royal and the construction of a new variety theatre and circus.

Frank Matcham, the leading theatre architect of his day, was engaged to design the new theatre. His surviving works include the interior of the London Palladium, the Manchester Palace and the Tower Ballroom in Blackpool. Building work was carried out by Thomas Godwin of Hanley, who later built other Matcham works around the country. Originally advertised as opening in October 1897, it took another ten months until the building was ready[286].

The entrance to the building was located on the corner of Trinity Street and Foundry Street and built of red brick in the Renaissance style, similar in looks to that of the Blackpool Grand. A large dome stood at the top of the building, and waiting patrons were protected from the elements with an iron and glass awning. The stage and auditorium walls extended down Foundry Street and Lower Foundry Street.

The auditorium could seat 2,594 people; 100 in the orchestra stalls, 240 in the pit stalls, 750 in the pit, 172 in the dress circle, 468 in the upper circle, and 864 in the gallery. Up to 4,000 could be accommodated when standing room in the pit and gallery was taken into account. The dress circle had four rows of gilded chairs upholstered in gold Utrecht velvet whilst the upper circle, on the same level and to the rear of the dress, contained a saloon. It also possessed restricted views due to the iron columns supporting the gallery above. Further seating was provided in four boxes to the sides of the circle. The general decoration was in shades of cream and gold, with further painted decoration on the ceiling and proscenium by Signor Buccini, along with busts of Shakespeare and Goethe. In order to keep the air in the theatre fresh, a sliding roof was installed for ventilation.

The stage was 63ft wide and 44ft deep, with a proscenium opening of 36ft. This could be widened to 41ft, with each side of the proscenium able to be swung back on a hinge mechanism allowing the use of the stage by circus acts. A circus arena could be formed by lowering sections of the stage into a well and encroaching into the front of the stalls. A scene dock and property room was constructed on stage right, measuring 40ft by 16ft.

The inner entrance hall contained marble columns, encaustic floor tiles and a decorated ceiling; with the rest of the rooms decorated on a "lavish scale". Refreshment rooms, lavatories and retiring rooms were also provided for the audience.

In case of fire, ample exits for evacuation were provided along with fireproof doors and stairs throughout. Steel and cement were also used extensively for the same reason, with fire hydrants and buckets installed on every floor[287].

On Monday 22nd August 1898, in the midst of a heatwave, a "large and enthusiastic crowd" gathered for the opening night's entertainments[288]. At 7.30pm Miss. Lilian Lea and the company sang the national anthem, accompanied by the fifteen piece band led by Morace Bianci. The acts on opening night included Miss. Lea, Professor John Higgins - the "human kangaroo", the Anglos Trio performing their 'Globe Walking', The Valdares, along with comedian Harry Tate.

Manager Frank Allen thanked those present on behalf of the Elphinstones, and hoped that the Grand would prove "a credit to the town." Seats would cost 6d in the pit, 2s in the stalls, 1s 6d in the circle, 9d in the second circle and 3d in the gallery. A private box could be reserved for £1 1s.

The Grand Theatre of Varieties operated as a variety house, playing two shows nightly. The new 'moving pictures' were incorporated into the bill from very early in the theatre's life, with the frequent attraction of the "Grand Pictures". In the week of 15th November 1909, this consisted of a presentation of "Nero, or the Burning of Rome." The theatre would also be transformed into a circus with travelling circuses taking over the theatre for a week or two at the time.

Old Theatres in the Potteries

Photo © Victoria and Albert Museum, London

In the early years of the theatre, George Cooke was employed as the resident caricaturist. In his many illustrations he drew the many names in variety visiting Hanley. These included Juno Salmo 'The Golden Mephisto' - an acrobat in a golden frog costume, Woody Kelly - the whiskered tramp, comedian Will Manning, and Dr. Carl Hermann- "The Man Who Tamed Electricity!"[289]. Cooke later moved to the Palace in Blackpool, located next to Blackpool Tower, and later to London.

Above. George Cooke's drawing of Fred Conquest in 'The Freak's Revenge' at the Grand Theatre of Varieties, Hanley, week beginning 22nd April 1907. The act entailed the freak monkey man taking revenge on the man who took away his wife and daughter.

99

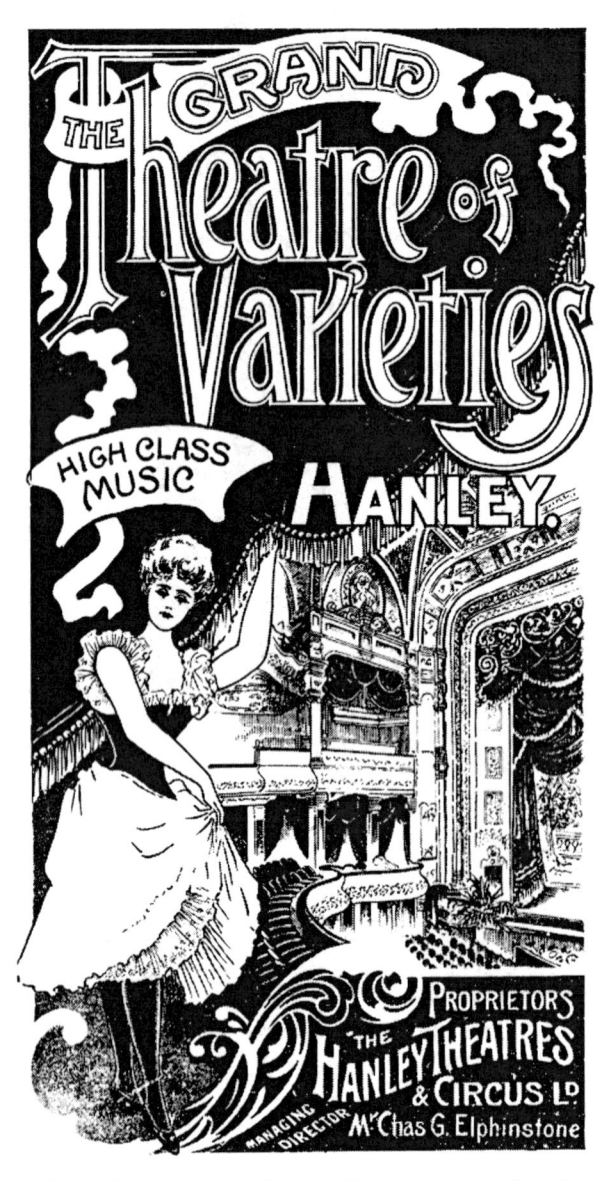

Above. Front cover of a 1909 programme for the Grand, showing the auditorium.

PROGRAMME

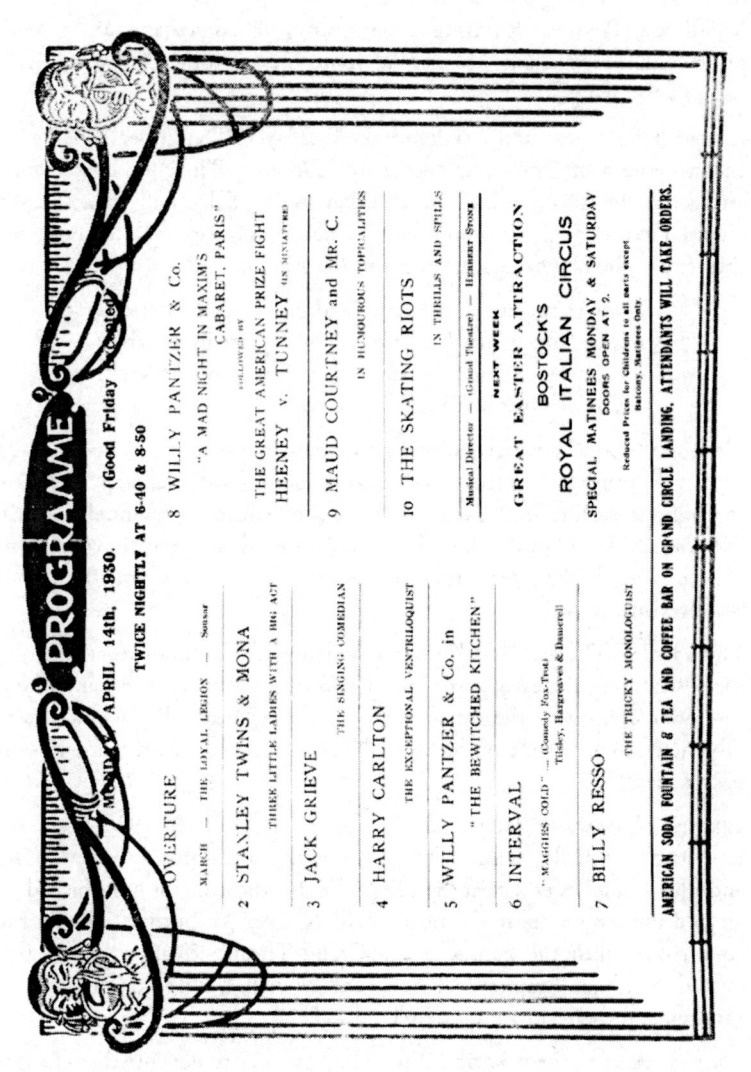

MONDAY, APRIL 14th, 1930. (Good Friday Excepted)

TWICE NIGHTLY AT 6-40 & 8-50

1 OVERTURE
    MARCH — THE LOYAL LEGION — Sousa

2 STANLEY TWINS & MONA
    THREE LITTLE LADIES WITH A BIG ACT

3 JACK GRIEVE
    THE SINGING COMEDIAN

4 HARRY CARLTON
    THE EXCEPTIONAL VENTRILOQUIST

5 WILLY PANTZER & Co. in
    "THE BEWITCHED KITCHEN"

6 INTERVAL
    "MAGGIE'S COLD" (Comedy Fox-Trot)
    Thisky, Hargreaves & Damerell

7 BILLY RESSO
    THE TRICKY MONOLOQUIST

8 WILLY PANTZER & Co.
    "A MAD NIGHT IN MAXIM'S CABARET, PARIS"
    FOLLOWED BY
    THE GREAT AMERICAN PRIZE FIGHT
    HEENEY v. TUNNEY (IN MINIATURE)

9 MAUD COURTNEY and Mr. C.
    IN HUMOUROUS TOPICALITIES

10 THE SKATING RIOTS
    IN THRILLS AND SPILLS

Musical Director — (Grand Theatre) — HERBERT STONE

NEXT WEEK
GREAT EASTER ATTRACTION
BOSTOCK'S
ROYAL ITALIAN CIRCUS
SPECIAL MATINEES MONDAY & SATURDAY
DOORS OPEN AT 2.
Reduced Prices for Children to all parts except
Balcony, Matinees Only

AMERICAN SODA FOUNTAIN & TEA AND COFFEE BAR ON GRAND CIRCLE LANDING. ATTENDANTS WILL TAKE ORDERS.

Above. The bill for a night's entertainment at the Grand in the week of 14th April 1930.

Charlie Chaplin appeared at the Grand on at least two occasions, the second was in the week beginning 30th November 1908 where he played the villain in Fred Karno's comedy sketch "The Football Match". It depicted a humourous battle between the Midnight Wanderers and Middleton Piecans, featuring a company of comedians along with professional footballers[290]. Chaplin went on to tour the world with Karno's company[291].

Arnold Bennett was in the audience on Tuesday 7th December 1909[292]. He encountered a bill including the Dainty Doretta - "juvenile comedienne and acrobatic sabot dancer", ju jitsu dancing by Falco and Eida and the Grand Pictures with Cummin and Seaham[293]. He later wrote about the theatre as 'The Hanbridge Empire' for *The Nation:*

> "Now I saw an immense carved and gilded interior, not as large as the Paris Opéra, but assuredly capable of seating as many persons. My first thought was: "Why, it's just like a real music-hall![294]"

Although built as a variety theatre and circus, the Grand was occasionally used for musical comedy and drama along with charity concerts throughout its life. In 1906 the Countess of Lathom presented the play 'Diplomacy' in aid of the Potteries Cripples Guild. The theatre would also play host to similar events for The Sentinel Penny Fund and the North Stafford Infirmary[295].

The Hanley Theatres and Circus Company had planned to reorganise their theatres in the early part of the 1910s by converting the Grand into a venue for 'legitimate' theatre and rebuilding the Theatre Royal as a theatre of varieties, however the outbreak of the great war stopped the progression of this plan[296].

Charles Elphinstone later sold the theatre in October 1920 upon his retirement, with the venue coming under the ownership of Alan Young and the Manchester Palace Syndicate[297]. The theatre was refurbished at around the same time to the plans of W. & T. R. Milburn[298]. The theatre later passed into the hands of the Grand Theatre (Hanley) Ltd, 50% owned by Moss Empires, 41% by the Manchester Palace of Varieties Limited and the rest by local shareholders[299].

For nine years in the twenties, Percy Hughes, later to become the manager of the Theatre Royal, served as assistant manager under manager H.J. Crane.

With the popularity of variety on the decline and with the success of the new talking pictures, it was decided by the owners that the theatre would become a cinema. The administration would be handled by H.D. Moorhouse of Manchester and in February 1932, the Grand opened as a full-time cinema equipped for sound. The first film shown was 'Sally in Our Alley' starring Gracie Fields, who addressed the audience by telephone from her dressing room at the Opera House, Blackpool on opening night[300]. A new manager was appointed the following month from the Manchester Hippodrome, George Henry Barrasford[301].

In the early hours of the 11th May 1932, mere months after conversion into a cinema, a mysterious fire gutted the auditorium and stage of the building. The fire was first seen at around 5.30am by two passing motorists who promptly raised the alarm with Hanley Fire Brigade. Manager Barrasford was resident at the time in the apartments in the front of the building with his wife, child and maid. After an attempt to reach the gallery of the theatre, where he was beaten back by the smoke and flames, he rescued the records from the office before fleeing with his family.

Four fire engines and thirty-five members of the fire brigade came to the scene, utilising the neighbouring *Evening Sentinel* offices as a vantage point. Shortly after 6am the roof of the auditorium collapsed down into the stalls, sending a tower of flames and sparks into the Hanley sky. Firefighters attempted to bring the fire under control and to prevent the fire from spreading to the neighbouring industrial premises, however just three hours after the initial sighting of smoke, another collapse brought down the roof onto the stage, sealing the theatre's fate.

By noon the following day, the fire was extinguished. A heap of twisted girders, smouldering beams and smashed plasterwork were all that remained of the auditorium. The front part of the building housing the foyer, apartments and booking office escaped the flames but suffered from the amount of water poured onto the theatre. Thirty six people were working at the theatre at the time of the fire, and were thus made redundant[302].

This was not the first fire to hit the theatre. A small fire in the early twenties had destroyed two rows of seats, and a second later that decade started in the Grand Circle and almost spread throughout the other tiers. Both of these were quickly extinguished and performances were not affected.

The empty shell stood derelict for several years, however there were plans to reconstruct the theatre. In 1934 a local syndicate headed by James Grant purchased the ruins of the theatre, aiming to construct a 2,000 seater variety theatre on behalf of a London syndicate[303]. This plan did not come to fruition and the site was subsequently sold to the Odeon company.

In 1937 a new, art-deco Odeon Cinema was opened on the site, designed by Harry Weedon and possessing limited stage facilities[304]. This venue closed in 1975 when operators C.M.A. downsized their operation in the city, keeping just the triple-screened Gaumont open. The building was used for storage until the early 2000s when the auditorium was converted into the 'Chicago Rock Cafe', a nightclub. The foyer was also converted into a bar, appropriately titled 'The Foyer', before it became a branch of the nationwide vodka bar chain, 'Revolution'.

Above. The site of the Grand Theatre in 2010. The land was used to construct the Odeon cinema in 1937, which now holds the Chicago Rock Cafe and a branch of Revolution.

Regent Theatre, Hanley

The Regent Theatre is located on Piccadilly, Hanley, between Cheapside and Pall Mall.

The building was commissioned by Provincial Cinematograph Theatres; one of many built by the company including other Regents in Bournemouth, Brighton and Bristol and the New Victoria in London, now the Apollo Victoria Theatre. Hanley was chosen as a location, according to the souvenir programme, due to Arnold Bennett's description of the town as being the "Chicago of the Five Towns".

Designed by William E. Trent, building work commenced in January 1928 and took thirteen months to complete[305]. During construction a seam of coal was discovered towards the Pall Mall part of the site, not particularly surprising given the extent of coal mining in the area.

The cinema was constructed with around a million bricks, 500 tons of steel girders and 480 tons of cement. It was built on two levels, stalls on the ground floor holding 1,372 and a balcony holding 812, giving a total capacity of 2,184[306]. Internal decoration was in the "modern French" style, with decorative plaster mouldings and a large dome above the stalls. A "multicolour system" was also installed which could flood the auditorium with a variety of fading colours. Pipes for a Wurlitzer organ were installed around the proscenium, controlled by a 2 Manual/9 Rank console on a hydraulic lift in the orchestra pit. This would ascend into full view of the audience for organ solos. The resident organist at the time of opening was E. Felton Rapley.

Not constructed just as a cinema, the Regent was constructed with full facilities to allow stage productions to take place. The stage house was located on Pall Mall, with the auditorium running almost parallel to Piccadilly.

The entrance from Piccadilly was clad in white glazed terracotta and upon entering through the etched glass doors, patrons were met by a spacious entrance hall. This was decorated with a chequered marble floor, plaster mouldings and a frieze painted by D. Barnes of 'Pottery in the East'. A mirror-walled cafe was located on the first floor capable of seating 300, itself decorated with doric columns and further plasterwork.

Above. The entrance to the Regent Theatre, Hanley in 2010.

The cinema was opened on Monday 11th February 1929 by the Lord and Lady Mayoress of Stoke-on-Trent William T. Leason and wife. The opening film was 'The Last Command' starring Emil Jannings and Evelyn Brent, telling the story of a Czarist General reduced to poverty after the collapse of Imperial Russia. Accompanying the film was a variety show entitled 'Something Different', starring the nine Regent Girls who travelled around the various cinemas in the chain. Comedy dancers Graham and Douglas and soprano Theresa Walters joined them, along with E. Felton Rapley on the organ and the pit orchestra led by Mr Clarke-Burne. In the same month that the Regent opened PCT was acquired by the Gaumont-British group, although it continued to operate under the Regent name.

July 1929 saw the first 'talkies' in the Potteries premiered at the Regent, with Al Jolson in 'The Singing Fool'. With the advent of the longer-running talking pictures there was less need to present acts between the short features, however they were still occasionally produced.

The Regent, already owned by Gaumont-British, was renamed on 24th September 1950 to become the Gaumont. Following the conversion of the nearby Theatre Royal into a bingo hall in 1961 and its complete closure to theatrical groups in 1966, the Gaumont became the only large, proscenium stage in operation in the city. The owners opened it up for booking by the local amateur societies, with the City of Stoke-on-Trent Amateur Operatic Society and the Newcastle Amateur Operatic Society being the main users. Over the years they presented such musicals as 'The Most Happy Fella', 'The Desert Song', 'My Fair Lady' and 'The Merry Widow'. The Gaumont also staged professional pantomimes, starting with Gerry and the Pacemakers in 'Babes in the Wood' in 1963.

The same year also saw a concert by teenage singer Helen Shapiro, supported by a then-unknown band from Liverpool, The Beatles. The biggest pop names appeared in the sixties and seventies, included Shirley Bassey, Matt Monro, Roy Orbison, Stevie Wonder, and Cliff Richard. During one of the visits from the Rolling Stones an outbreak of hysteria caused thirty five girls to lose consciousness. The Wurlitzer organ was removed in 1972 and is believed to now be broken up[307]. The original cafe had by then closed and replaced by a dancing school.

Following the introduction of television in the area, especially independent television in 1956, the number of cinema goers had dwindled, causing many venues to close. The larger chains began to convert their larger venues into multiple screens to offer an increased choice. The Gaumont was split into three using the 'drop-wall' method, where the area underneath the circle was walled off and two small cinemas constructed in the space. Fortunately this method was relatively non-destructive to the interior decoration as some other cinemas of the time were totally gutted to allow conversion.

On Sunday 12th May 1974 the building reopened as the Gaumont Film Centre. Screen 1 was the original auditorium, with the front stalls and circle seating around 1,350, and Screens 2 and 3 were located under the balcony holding 150 each. The Gaumont was later renamed the 'Odeon' in June 1976, the name transferring from the Odeon in Trinity Street which had closed the previous year.

Live shows continued, including those from the local amateurs, who split their shows between the Odeon, Queen's Theatre in Burslem, and the Theatre Royal after its reopening in 1982. £500,000 was invested in the building in 1986 before the operations of the Odeon transferred to a new eight screen multiplex cinema on the new Festival Park in October 1989 The building was Grade II listed in the November[308] before standing empty for several years.

In the 1990s, local businessman Richard Talbot headed the 'Regent Theatre Trust' with the aim of restoring the building. He planned to reopen it as a multi-purpose arts centre, utilising all the facilities of the building[309]. The trust became a limited company in order to raise the £1,500,000 needed to restore and reopen the venue[310]. Time was of the essence; the ornamental dome had already succumbed to water damage from the leaking roof[311].

The council commissioned consultants 'The Art Business' to undertake an arts evaluation of the city, in particular looking at its theatre and concert hall facilities. It was of their opinion that the facilities in the city were sub-standard; the Victoria Hall being inadequately equipped with poor front-of-house facilities and no venue to take the top touring theatrical productions such as The Phantom of the Opera and Les Miserables, both having recently taken a long residence in Manchester[312]. A renovated Victoria Hall and Regent Theatre, along with the existing City Museum and Theatre Royal, new cafes, restaurants and wine bars would create a new concept, the 'Cultural Quarter'.

The council took over the project, unveiling plans and granting planning permission in late 1995[313]. The Regent would become a 1,600 seater theatre with up-to-date stage facilities to house touring shows, opera and ballet, whilst the Victoria Hall would be extended with new front-of-house facilities and improved facilities for artists. Funding was obtained from The National Lottery, the Arts Council, English Heritage, the City Council and the European Redevelopment Fund, and construction work began in 1996.

The architects for the renovation were Levitt Bernstein Associates. The rebuilding work on the Regent was immense; the years standing empty had taken its toll and the building was suffering from "damage and decay". The two additional cinemas under the balcony were removed and the stage and fly tower demolished, along with neighbouring buildings in Pall Mall. The proscenium arch was removed as was the first set of boxes in the auditorium, shrinking its depth. This would enable a larger stage house to be constructed. Before this could be done however the Spencroft and Great Row coal seams beneath the site had to be stabilised by injecting concrete into the workings. A new replica proscenium was constructed further into the auditorium and the other plasterwork was restored, particularly the dome, at a cost of £400,000[314]. The new fly tower, an imposing sight on the Hanley skyline, was covered in 1100m^2 of terracotta rain screening and emblazoned with the theatre name[315]. The front of house facilities were totally reconstructed, including replacing the former dancing school with the 'Britannia Suite', a new hospitality suite to hold 200. The Piccadilly facade was refreshed, with new glass doors installed along with a new glass awning. Disabled access was provided throughout the refurbished venue.

The completed venue would hold 1,615, with 901 in the stalls and 714 in the circle, including 24 wheelchair spaces. The front rows of seats in the stalls could also be removed to allow for an enlarged orchestra pit. Bars and toilets were provided on all levels of the theatre for the use of patrons. The Ambassador Theatre Group were engaged to operate the venue on behalf of the council.

The new stage was 99ft wide, varying in depth from 44ft stage right to 52 ft stage left, with a 41ft wide proscenium. Provision was made for connection to an external ice plant, allowing the staging of ice shows, and full facilities for flying scenery up into the tower. Thirteen dressing rooms were available to hold 74 artists, and two band rooms for up to thirty musicians[316].

Old Theatres in the Potteries

Above. The new fly tower of the Regent Theatre in Pall Mall, Hanley. Constructed as part of renovations in 1998/9.

The work did not go smoothly however. Workmen downed tools when the architects failed to be paid by Stoke-on-Trent City Council. Work eventually restarted but after a fifteen month arbitration case, the originally budgeted £4.7 million for the refurbishment of both venues rose to around £20 million. This included the associated legal fees which Stoke-on-Trent City Council had to pay[317].

The first production on the new stage was on the evening of Friday 17th September 1999 when the Porthill Players presented 'Songs from the Shows'. The following Tuesday, the 22nd September 1999, the venue was reopened with the national tour of 'Annie' starring Lesley Joseph. Sir Derek Jacobi performed the opening ceremony the following day, paying tribute in his speech to former council leader Ted Smith, instrumental in the development of the Cultural Quarter[318]. The building was finally opened officially by Her Majesty The Queen on Thursday 28th October during her visit to the city, unveiling a plaque in the foyer.

Since reopening, the theatre has presented the national tours of Cats, Starlight Express, Doctor Dolittle, Noises Off, Jesus Christ Superstar, Whistle Down the Wind, Matthew Bourne's Swan Lake, Calendar Girls, Guys and Dolls, and An Inspector Calls to name but a handful. Unfortunately it has yet to attract the long residencies of musicals fresh from London that prompted its conversion.

The Glyndebourne Touring Opera moved its productions from Manchester to the theatre in 1999, and has returned each year. The local amateur societies have also frequently booked the venue, presenting shows such as Rent, Scrooge, and The Producers. Since 2005, Jonathan Wilkes has starred in the annual pantomime, receiving record attendances.

It took seven years for Regent Theatre and Victoria Hall to turn a profit, generating £31,346 in the year to September 2006. Sadly the venues returned to losing money the following year. The council subsidises the venues at a cost of £500,000 per annum, set in 2007 and rising each year with inflation[319].

The theatre celebrated its tenth and eightieth anniversary in 2009, with the Ambassador Theatre Group continuing with the management of the venue for many years to come.

Century Theatre, Hanley

The Century Theatre was a travelling theatre founded in 1948 by John Ridley. It first visited the Potteries in 1952 whilst touring to nineteen other towns between Burnley and Stafford. The theatre itself comprised of four lorries raised into position to provide a sloping floor, with "comfortable", air-conditioned seating for 225. The company comprised of sixteen actors and stage hands, and accommodation was provided for them as part of the travelling entourage[320].

One member of the company was Eileen Derbyshire, later to play Emily Bishop in Coronation Street[321]. In June 1960, the visiting company made its fourth visit to Hanley and set up behind the museum in Broad Street, Hanley. 'Uncle Vanya' was performed on opening night to a disappointing audience of just twelve. 'Mr Belfry' and 'Look Back in Anger' were due to be staged during the rest of the fortnight long engagement[322].

Mitchell Memorial Theatre, Hanley

The Mitchell Memorial Theatre, Broad Street, Hanley, was opened in 1957 as a tribute to designer of the Spitfire, Reginald Mitchell. An appeal had been launched in 1943 to fund such a memorial.

At a charity film showing the Lord Mayor, C. Austin Brook, stated that he believed "the best memorial which could be given was one which could help the youth of the country to tackle the jobs which would be theirs in the future."[323] The Spitfire Mitchell Memorial Fund was set up to provide and maintain a "centre for the education and recreation of persons of both sexes up to the age of 20 years and other ancillary purposes." Plans were put on show in 1947 and the foundation stone laid in May 1955 after fundraising efforts.

The auditorium could hold 382 in what was "a dual-purpose auditorium". This meant that the floor could be pivoted between flat and raked positions, and the seating removed to give space for "dancing and social occasions", along with theatrical productions[324]. The stage was 28ft wide and 24ft deep with a 5ft apron projecting into the auditorium[325]. An orchestra pit could be formed by removing the first few rows of seating. The architects were the firm of Wood, Goldstraw and Yorath, with P. Bailey of Hanford carrying out construction work.

The first event in the new hall was the annual presentation of the Stoke-on-Trent and District School Sports Association, on Wednesday 23rd October 1957. The opening ceremony was performed by famed Battle of Britain pilot Douglas Bader on Monday 28th October, when a biopic film of the life of Reginald Mitchell, 'The First of the Few', was shown. For the event, the building was floodlit using searchlights from local anti-aircraft units to form a cone of light over the building. At opening the building was the 'Spitfire Mitchell Memorial Youth Centre'.

Over the years the building has been home to many of the amateur theatre societies in the area, along with local dance groups, youth groups, and productions from the local education committee.

The venue closed in April 2009 for a major refurbishment, following the transfer of the building and adjoining Cartwright House to a new charitable trust. New dressing rooms, a cafe, improved backstage facilities and a specialist dance studio will be constructed, costing in the region of £4,000,000. When reopened, it will be renamed the 'Mitchell Memorial Youth Art Theatre'[326].

Above. The exterior of the Mitchell Memorial Youth Art Theatre during rebuilding work in 2010.

Victoria Theatre, Hartshill

The Victoria Theatre was located on the corner of Hartshill Road and Victoria Street, in Hartshill.

Stephen Joseph was a pioneer of theatre-in-the-round, stating

> "the picture-frame stage, no matter how glorious its past, has never had much connection with the drama, and it is now an incubus which is suffocating live entertainment."[327]

Joseph was the son of actress Hermione Gingold and publisher Michael Joseph, and founded his Studio Theatre Company in 1955 to present theatre-in-the-round in Scarborough and on tour around the country. In 1959 the Municipal Hall in Newcastle-under-Lyme was included on the tour route, returning in 1960[328].

At the time Newcastle had no theatre of its own, the Newcastle and Pottery Theatre having closed many decades previously. Plans had been developing since 1946 for the construction of a new civic theatre which had not yet come to fruition. The Municipal Hall had served on several occasions as a proscenium arch theatre but this was not a permanent or ideal arrangement, possessing as it did a flat floor. The successful engagements of the Studio Theatre Company with their portable bleacher seating reawakened the idea of a civic theatre for Newcastle.

Newcastle Borough Council investigated reopening the derelict Theatre Royal before plans were drawn up for a new theatre-in-the-round to be constructed on the Brampton, designed by Stephen Garrett. It would seat 400, have a 24ft diameter stage in the round and cost £60,000. The Studio Theatre Company would have used the theatre as their new base of operations, however development was delayed and subsequently never constructed[329].

Whilst awaiting decision on the new Brampton theatre, Joseph's company moved into the Victoria Theatre in Hartshill. Opened in 1913 it had served as a cinema for many years, operating as a cine-variety venue during the silent era. It closed in July 1960 due to "pathetically low" audiences resulting from the spread of television[330].

Old Theatres in the Potteries

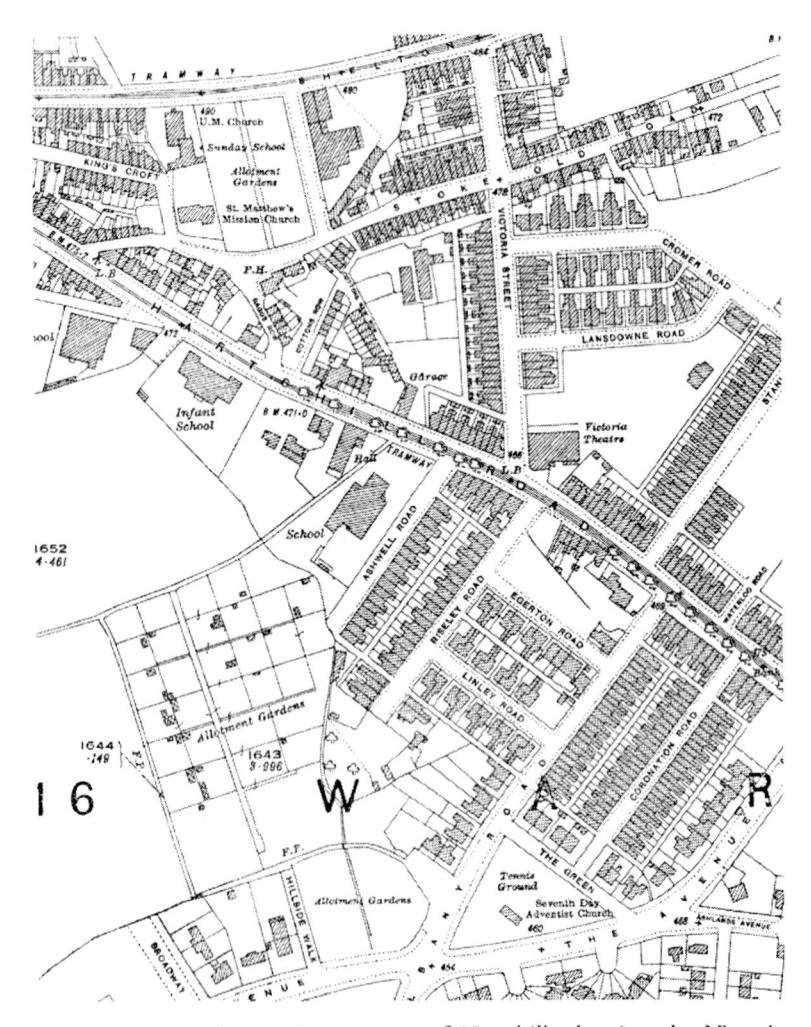

Above. 1920s Ordnance Survey map of Hartshill, showing the Victoria Theatre on the corner of Hartshill Road and Victoria Street, as a cinema.

In 1961 the building was converted into North Staffordshire's first nightclub. The sloping floor was levelled to become a tiered dining area and a maple dance floor installed, with music coming from a state-of-the-art electronic organ. 'The Victoria Theatre Club' opened on Friday 19th May 1961 presenting "top-class" cabaret, dancing and tombola, and would stay open as late as 11.30pm![331] Wrestling was also a feature on selected nights. The venture was not a success and its licence was removed making it available for Stephen Joseph to lease in August of 1962.

The building was converted in two phases, the second to come when further money was available. The initial funding came from several sources; £2,500 from actor William Elmhurst, £250 from a public appeal and £700 from weekend independent television contractor ABC. Granada Television also agreed to help, footing the bill for the installation of the seats in the venue.

The conversion was overseen by architect Peter Fisher. The 24ft x 22ft rectangular stage was surrounded on four sides by 345 tiered seats, each row 1ft 3inchs higher than the one below. A large technical control room was built at one end with makeshift electronic equipment.

The work was complete in just three weeks and Tuesday 9th October 1962 saw the opening of the theatre. The first production was 'The Birds and the Wellwishers' by William Norfolk, starring a then-unknown Alan Ayckbourn along with Heather Stoney. The play was directed by Peter Cheeseman.

In the first six weeks after opening audiences were low, averaging 33% of capacity, around half that needed to make a profit. Despite the lack of immediate financial success the second phase of the conversion began in November of 1962. Costing another £5,000, the auditorium was decorated and the lighting, sound and acoustics improved.

The theatre put a great deal of effort into giving talks and lectures to local people regarding the theatre, visiting schools, colleges and clubs, which continues today at the New Victoria in the Borderlines scheme[332].

In 1965 an Arts Council grant enabled the Vic to take on a resident dramatist. Worcester schoolteacher Peter Patterson was appointed and became known as Peter Terson. His play 'The Mighty Reservoy' had been presented the previous year. His later works at the Vic included 'All Honour Mr. Todd' (1966), 'I'm In Charge of these Ruins' (1966), 'The Ballad of Artificial Mash' (1967), '1861 Whitby Lifeboat Disaster' (1970) and 'But Fred Freud is Dead' (1972).

Over the years, the theatre launched the careers of several famous actors. Robert Powell, known to millions as 'Jesus of Nazareth', and Ben Kingsley, winner of the Oscar for playing 'Gandhi', began their careers in Hartshill. Another member of the company was Edward Clayton, who for many years appeared as Stan Harvey in the ATV soap opera 'Crossroads'. Bob Hoskins was part of the company for a time, appearing in 'Romeo and Juliet' in March 1968. Roy Barraclough also played at the Vic, later to star along side Les Dawson and as Alec Gilroy in 'Coronation Street'[333]. Carol Drinkwater was also in the company for a time.

The Victoria Theatre gained a strong reputation for staging local musical-documentaries. The first presented was 'The Jolly Potters' in 1964, concerning the pottery industry in the 1840s. 'The Staffordshire Rebels' came next in 1965 about the English civil war. The most acclaimed and successful was 'The Knotty' in 1966, telling the story of the North Staffordshire Railway. 'The Knotty' was such a success that it was revived four times, in 1967, 1969, 1978 and 2008[334]. It also toured to the International Festival of Permanent Theatre Companies in Florence, Italy in April 1969[335].

Further musical documentaries followed, 'Six into One' in 1968 relating to the federation of the six towns of the Potteries, 'The Burning Mountain' in 1970, this time about founder of the Primitive Methodists Hugh Bourne, and 'Hands Up – for you the war is ended' in 1971 concerning the local loss of life in the First World War.

In April 1966 the subsidy awarded to the theatre was doubled to £15,000 per year and Stephen Joseph wished to appoint two further theatre directors to share Cheeseman's workload, promoting him to the position of Artistic Director. Cheeseman was unhappy with this plan and his refusal to accept the new post eventually resulting in his barring from the theatre at the end of his contract in January 1967[336]. Joseph said at the time "that over the past four years, the Victoria Theatre has become firmly established and that now is the time to plan further development." He also accused Cheeseman of attempting to take over the board[337].

Cheeseman was still in the process of directing "She Stoops to Conquer" and "Julius Caesar" at the time of his barring, having to complete the work in a nearby public house[338]. Students at Keele University started a petition to get Cheeseman reinstated and dedicated an edition of the student paper to the cause.

After much discussion, it was announced that the board of Studio Theatre would be willing to hand over the control of the theatre to a new local trust, with the support of the Arts Council.

Stoke-on-Trent City Council attempted to form a trust to take the building over but Joseph declined, preferring to deal with Newcastle-under-Lyme[339]. As the future became more uncertain, grants from other local councils, including Biddulph, started to dry up.

Whilst unemployed, Cheeseman directed his production of 'Jock-on-the-Go' by Peter Terson for BBC Television in the Midlands[340], featuring the original cast members from the Vic. The pair also produced an adaptation of the Arnold Bennett work 'The Heroism of Thomas Chadwick' for ABC Weekend Television, again with members of the company. As a result, Joseph instructed his solicitors to apply for an injunction to prevent Cheeseman from "enticing" away the company of the Vic[341].

The entire acting company resigned at the start of April, along with resident dramatist Peter Terson and three technicians[342]. Business manager Vyvian Nixon and assistant director Joyce Cheeseman were also sacked by the Studio Theatre. Stephen Joseph was at this time at his home in Scarborough, fighting the cancer that would eventually take his life in October 1967.

A complete new team of actors were recruited under the hand of new artistic director Terry Lane. These included a young Tony Robinson, now famous for appearing in the BBC's 'Blackadder' and Channel 4's 'Time Team'. During his time in Stoke he played a villager in a production of Ibsen's 'Brand', directed by Raymond Ross.[343]

By May 1967 it was agreed that the Stoke-on-Trent and North Staffordshire Theatre Trust would takeover the assets of the theatre from Joseph[344], offering to pay £5,000. An extra £3,000 was granted to the Vic to keep it running until the transfer took place[345].

The trust, chaired by Sir Albert Bennett, took control of the theatre on 3th July[346]. One of the tasks of the new trust was to appoint a new artistic director and out of over thirty applicants Peter Cheeseman was chosen[347], with Vyvian Nixon returning as business manager.

The Vic reopened on 5th September 1967 with 'The Ballad of the Artificial Mash', the sixth play by Peter Terson. The play told the story of Norman Dodd, a seller of artificial animal feed who succumbed to the hormones in the product he sold and changed gender. Reviews were not kind[348], however it was later dramatised for ABC Weekend Television starring Stanley Holloway.

The foyer of the theatre was used as an art gallery from time to time; paintings by Lady Trevelyan were exhibited in 1967[349], and works by Arthur Berry were exhibited in 1979.

The year 1969/70 saw a twenty percent increase in attendances and the most successful financial year in the history of the company. An average of 65% of seats were sold and over 70,000 seats were sold during the year. This was cited as reason for advancing with plans for the construction of a new building, along with the lack of facilities at the Hartshill site. Actors were housed in two, small dressing rooms and the workshop where new sets, costumes and props were constructed was small and inadequate. A temporary solution to the increased attendances was created with the addition of 47 extra seats in 1971.

1973 saw 'Fight for Shelton Bar', a new documentary based on the then-current struggle to prevent the closure of Shelton steelworks. An adaptation of the production was recorded by BBC Pebble Mill for the 'Second City First' series. Further documentaries followed, 'Awkward Cuss'- 1976's look at the life of Havergal Brian and 1980's 'Plain Jos', detailing the life of Josiah Wedgwood.

The theatre also showcased a large number of stage adaptations of the work of Arnold Bennett, adapted by Peter Terson and Joyce Cheeseman. These included Clayhanger, Jock-on-the-Go, The Old Wive's Tale, Anna of the Five Towns, and The Card.

A new theatre at last

Following the aborted sixties Brampton theatre, efforts were relaunched to find a more appropriate home for the Vic company. A dozen sites in Stoke-on-Trent were initially offered to the theatre in the early seventies, none of went any further. A location in Broad Street was shortlisted, which would have given an early version of the Cultural Quarter comprising of the ABC Cinebowl, Mitchell Memorial Theatre and New Victoria Theatre[350], however Unity House was eventually built on the site.

The next choice was land at the entrance of the new Hanley Forest Park but negotiations with the landlord failed. Another twenty sites were offered in 1974, with one at Hartshill being chosen[351]. This was refused by the city council, and both councils offered further sites. Stoke offered a car park in Vale Street, Stoke, land to the rear of the Victoria Hall, Hanley, and Queensway at Longport[352], whilst Newcastle Borough Council offered Rosendale on the Brampton and a 2½ acre site at Stoneyfields on Etruria Road[353]. After months of deliberation the site at Stoneyfields was chosen, rented for 125 years at a very low rent. The reasons given for choosing the site were due to its centrality to the district and its high density of trees[354].

The recession in the early eighties delayed construction of the new 650 seater theatre whilst the £3,200,000 needed were raised. £750,000 was pledged by Staffordshire County Council in 1982 and £640,000 of Arts Council funding came through in April 1983[355]. The two councils then announced their commitments, Stoke-on-Trent giving £400,625 and Newcastle-under-Lyme £400,000, with Staffordshire Moorlands District Council donating £3000[356]. The remaining £750,000 was left for the theatre to raise, with an appeal team led by Joan Levitt.

The plans were put on display in December 1983. John Sambrook's auditorium was constructed around a super-elliptical stage, not much larger than that at the Vic but with increased seating for 600, all within 26ft of the stage. Large dressing rooms were to be provided for the artistes, along with toilets and showers, a staff sitting room, rehearsal rooms, workshops, a wardrobe department and plenty of store rooms. Patrons would have the use of a large foyer, a bar, book store, coffee shop, self-service restaurant and the 'Stephen Joseph Room', a smaller venue.

The first sod was cut in May 1984 by key backer Sir George Wade in a ceremony involving the acting company, who provided a short play[357]. In order to give the management and creative team time to prepare for the new theatre, the old Vic closed on 9 March 1985 with 'The Victoria Theatre's Forward Looking Nostalgia Show'[358]. The audience were joined by former members of the company including Heather Stoney and Robert Powell.

The New Victoria Theatre finally opened on 13th August 1986 with a production of local playwright Arthur Berry's play 'St. George of Scotia Road'.

The original Victoria Theatre building still stands in Hartshill today, partially reconstructed but is still visibly the same building, and is now home to shops and car parking spaces.

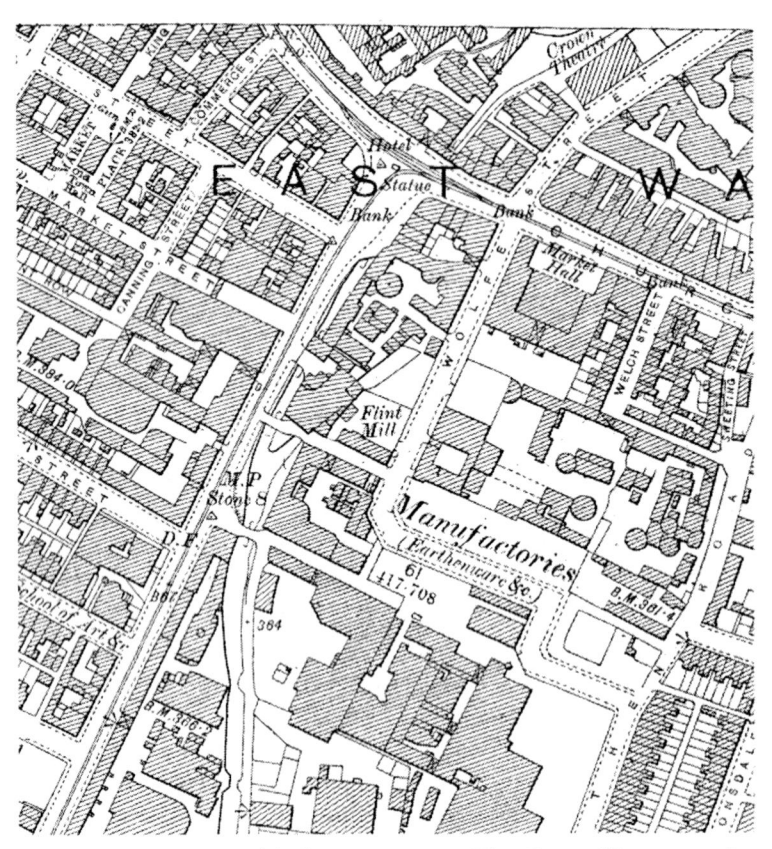

Above. 1900 OS Map of Stoke town centre. The Crown Theatre can be seen at the very top right of the map sandwiched between the canal and Wolfe Street.

Crown Theatre, Stoke

The Crown Theatre was located in Wolfe Street, Stoke, now Kingsway. The area was previously the location of wharves on the Newcastle canal.

The theatre was commissioned by Haldane Crichton and Arthur Roscoe Carlton, proprietors of theatres at Davenport, Glossop, and Walsall[359]. Designed by Lynam, Beckett and Lynam of Stoke and Hanley the building was constructed of wood and iron. It could hold 1,100 in total, 700 in the pit seated in tip-up seats and 400 in the balcony, along with the four private boxes. Refreshment rooms were provided for the audience[360].

The stage was 52ft wide and 32ft deep, with a 27ft proscenium opening. It was equipped with "up-to-date" fittings and was said to be able to accommodate almost any play travelling the country. An attached block of dressing rooms was also provided. Electric light was fitted throughout and the stage was illuminated by two 2,000 candle power arc lights, with another installed outside the venue. The electricity was generated onsite by a gas engine, and the total cost of construction was said to be £1,400[361].

The opening took place on Monday 15th February 1897 with Hardie and Van Leer's company in the pantomime 'Cinderella'. It was attended by local magistrates, aldermen, councillors and their wives, along with a large crowd, too large in fact for them all to gain admittance[362]. Prior to the performance the seventy strong company sang the national anthem, along with the audience. The pantomime, with a "judiciously selected" cast, concluded with a series of moving pictures from R. W. Paul's Cinematograph[363].

At the start of 1898 Carlton sold his share in the theatre to Crichton, leaving him the sole proprietor. The building was later purchased by David Harding Mountford in 1899 who subsequently dismantled and sold off the venue to make way for his new Gordon Theatre and Opera House[364].

Above. Illustration of the Gordon Theatre made prior to construction. From Fenns' Borough Almanck.

Gordon Theatre and Opera House, Stoke

The Gordon Theatre and Opera House was located in Wolfe Street, Stoke now Kingsway, on the site of the former Crown Theatre.

The Crown had been purchased by David Harding Mountford, proprietor of the nearby Gordon Hotel, now the White Star. At the license renewal for the Crown in February 1899 he announced his intention to replace the building with a new theatre of brick[365].

The designers of the new theatre were theatrical architects Owen and Ward of Birmingham, and construction work was carried out by Thomas Godwin of Hanley. The frontage faced Wolfe Street and was built of red Accrington brick with terracotta dressings. Above the facade were two dome-shaped cupolas, between which stood a gilded figure representing liberty. Further down the facade was a bust of General Gordon of the Khartoum and the theatre name carved in stone. An iron and glass awning ran the whole length of the building to protect patrons from the elements.

The auditorium ran parallel to the street and could accommodate 2,000 persons over three levels, with steel cantilevers supporting the two balconies to give uninterrupted views of the stage. The ceilings and gallery fronts were decorated with gilded plasterwork, and the drapery around the stage was of turquoise embossed fabric with the private boxes decorated in the same style. The building was carpeted throughout, blue velvet tip-up seats fitted and the walls of the auditorium dressed with Japanese wallpaper. The stage measured 42ft deep with a proscenium opening of 28ft 6in, with a fireproof curtain installed.

The walls of the foyer was adorned with large paintings by Minton painter Anton Boullemier, and the floor covered with Minton tiles. Cloakrooms, coffee lounges, winter gardens and a saloon were provided for visitors, accessed by staircases of white marble. The whole building was lit with electricity and the total construction work cost £15,000[366].

On opening night, Monday 12th March 1900, Ben Greet's company presented 'Belle of New York' before a large audience and was said to provide "an excellent evening's entertainment". Mountford made his appearance on stage at curtain call and thanked the audience for their patronage. The theatre was not totally complete by opening night with some finishing touches still to be made[367].

GORDON THEATRE & OPERA HOUSE, STOKE-ON-TRENT.

MR. F. R. BENSON'S SHAKESPEAREAN CO.

JAN. 27 TO FEB. 1, 1902.

PROGRAMME.

Monday	January 27th,	THE TAMING OF THE SHREW
Tuesday	. 28th,	THE MERCHANT OF VENICE
Wednesday	. 29th,	HENRY THE FIFTH
Thursday	. 30th,	HAMLET
Friday	. 31st,	THE TAMING OF THE SHREW
Saturday	February 1st,	RICHARD THE THIRD

MATINEE.

Thursday January 30th, . HENRY THE FIFTH

Doors open 6.30, commence at 7.30. Matinee: Doors open 1 p.m., commence at 2 p.m.

PRICES OF ADMISSION.

Private Boxes, £1 1s. Dress Circle, 3/- Stalls, 2/- Balcony, 1/6
Pit, 1 - Gallery, 6d. Early Doors to all parts.
Dress Circle, Stalls, and Balcony Half-price at 9 o'clock.

BOX OFFICE OPEN 11 to 1 DAILY (MR. HILL).

LATE TRAINS.

Stoke for Tunstall	9.43, 10.11, 10.41, & 11.1.
Longton	10.7, 10.30, 10.55
Longton, Normacot, Blyth Bridge, Cresswell, Leigh, and Uttoxeter	11.5 (Thursdays and Saturdays only).
Newcastle	10.32 & 11.10
Silverdale (Saturdays only)	11.10
Stoke for Leek and intermediate stations (except Fenton Manor)	10.57 (Thursdays and Saturdays only).
Trentham, Barlaston, and Stone	11 (Thursdays & Saturdays only).
Harecastle and Crewe	11.5
Totmonslow and Cheadle	11.5 (Saturdays only).

SPECIAL CARS to HANLEY and LONGTON every night after the Performance.

Previous Page. Programme from the Gordon Theatre for the week beginning 27th January 1902

Initially, the programme at the Gordon was of straight plays and operas however audiences failed to attend in the numbers expected. A show typical of those booked in at this time was an engagement of F. R. Benson's Shakespearean Company, as seen in the programme on the opposite page. The theatre was also used to provide the "non-church going class" with a religious service on "neutral territory". For three months at the start of 1901, Reverend G. Townsend of the Congregational Church catered for around 500 worshippers every Sunday[368].

By April 1902, variety acts were being booked into the theatre however these failed to attract the audiences from the Grand in Hanley. On Saturday, 9th April 1904, Mountford closed the doors of the Gordon for the last time[369].

Showman Pat Collins, originally from Bloxwich, took the building over shortly after. He was widely known in the area for his travelling fairgrounds in Wakes weeks. After a short refurbishment 'Collin's Hippodrome' reopened on Whit Monday, 23rd May 1904. Collins aimed to present first-rate variety and the opening week saw famous music-hall stars Marie Loftus and Nellie Watson, along with 'The Happy Japs'. There was also a demonstration of wireless telegraphy by 'The Marconis' and the evening concluded with Collin's Animatograph, with "The Cockney Sportsman" with Glaude Ginnette showing on the silver screen.

The theatre was a success and continued to engage stars such as Alec Hurley, husband of music hall star Marie Lloyd, Charles Coburn and even presented live elephants on the stage!

The week of Monday, 31st October 1904 saw a major international star arrive in Stoke-upon-Trent. Collins had engaged Eugene Stratton for an unprecedented salary of £200 a week, over £11,000 in today's money! Stratton was famed as a "coon singer" - blackening his face with makeup to do so. The many residents who could not obtain tickets for inside the theatre crowded around it, hoping to get a glimpse of the arriving star[370]. Stratton performed his two songs and was met with "vociferous" applause. Other acts on the bill that night were Fred Terry with another "coon song" and 'The Castles' with their dancing statues.

Above. Poster for Stratton's engagement at the Hippodrome. 1904

Old Theatres in the Potteries

HIPPODROME
STOKE-ON-TRENT.

Telephone 1297.
Telegrams: "Hippodrome, Stoke-on-Trent."

Proprietor ... ... **T. ALLAN EDWARDES.**
(Also of the Grand Theatre, Derby; Palace, Glossop; Pavilion, Newcastle-on-Tyne)

Acting Manager ... ... **WALTER BELLIAN.**

TWO PERFORMANCES NIGHTLY!
At 6-55 and 9.

Open Every Evening with a First=class Company.

TWO PERFORMANCES NIGHTLY!
At 6-55 and 9.

Open Every Evening with a First=class Company.

PROGRAMME
FOR WEEK COMMENCING MONDAY, SEPTEMBER 11th, 1916.

First Performance, 6-55, Doors open at 6-20.   Second Performance, 9 o'clock, Doors open at 8-40.
All Children must be paid for.   Children in arms not admitted.   The right of admission is reserved.
Seats not Guaranteed unless Booked.

PRICES OF ADMISSION:—
BOXES, 7/6 (Tax 6d.) 8/-; Single Seats, bookable in advance, 1/6 (Tax 2d.) 1/8. **DRESS CIRCLE**, 1/- (Tax 2d.) 1/2; Early Doors 1/3 (Tax 2d.) 1/5; Booked in advance 1/6 (Tax 2d.) 1/8. **SECOND CIRCLE AND STALLS**, 6d. (Tax 1d.) 7d.; Early Doors 9d. (Tax 2d.) 11d.; Booked in advance 1/- (Tax 2d.) 1/2. **PIT**, 4d. (Tax 1d.) 5d.; Early Doors 6d. (Tax 1d.) 7d. **GALLERY**, 2d. (Tax ½d.) 2½d.; Early Doors 3d. (Tax 1d.) 4d.

Seats Booked and Reserved for Dress Circle, Second Circle and Pit Stalls, at the Hippodrome, or by Telephone No. 1297, daily from 10 a.m. to 2 p.m.; and from 8 to 9 p.m.

Above. Cover of a programme for week beginning 11th September 1916, with an engagement of the Empire Grand Opera Company.

Above. Inside of a theatre programme for the Hippodrome September 1914

In December Pat Collins sold the building to T. Allen Edwardes, proprietor of a series of music halls in the East Midlands. The first show under new ownership in January 1905 featured Vesta Tilley, another star of the music hall era. Frank Macnaghten of the Macnaghten Vaudeville Circuit took over in 1909, reopening after a refurbishment on Monday 2nd August 1909. He continued as proprietor until 1911 when Edwardes returned.

The theatre reverted to including dramas and operas on its bill, with engagements of the Empire Grand Opera Company, plays including 'Nick Carter, Detective' and 'The Better Land', and Christmas pantomimes such as 'Little Miss Ragtime' in 1912 and 'Little Bo Peep' in 1913[371].

As with many theatres, business was hit hard by the competition from the new picture palaces. On Easter Monday 21st April 1919, the Hippodrome reopened as a full-time picture house with Lou Faversham and Barbara Castleton in 'The Silver King', and Charlie Chaplin in 'Shoulder Arms'. The advertising tagline stated -

> "Stoke's Super Cinema. Completely Reconstructed, Redecorated, Refurnished. Entirely New Scientific Cinema Installation. Perfect Pictures under Ideal Conditions."

After a spell operated by the Biocolor circuit, the theatre became part of the Gaumont-British group in the late 1920s, and was converted for sound in 1930.

Boxing Day of 1951 saw the closure of the Hippodrome for an extensive programme of renovations. The upper circle was removed, which was out of use for a year previous, whilst the circle and stalls were reseated and new projectors installed. A complete redecoration took place including a new, more streamlined look for the interior decorations which replaced the original plaster mouldings. The reopening took place on 28th July 1952 with a personal appearance of film star Terence Morgan and a showing of the film 'The Greatest Show on Earth'. At the same time, the cinema changed its name to the 'Gaumont'[372].

Despite a brief spell of success following the installation of Cinemascope, the Gaumont closed on 14th January 1961 and was demolished the following May[373]. The site in Kingsway is now occupied by a row of shops and council offices, previously housing an early Tesco branch in the seventies[374]. All trace of the past is not lost however, a plaque on the building gives the block's name – 'Gordon House'.

Above. The site of the Hippodrome in Kingsway, now home to 'Gordon House'.

Old Theatres in the Potteries

Above. View of the former Church of St. Simon and St. Jude on the corner of Beresford Road and College Road, Shelton. It served as the home of the Stoke-on-Trent Repertory Theatre from 1933-1997.

Repertory Theatre, Stoke

The early twenties saw the beginning of the Stoke-on-Trent Dramatic Society, with a performance of 'Caste' at the Empire Theatre, Longton. Following further productions in various venues, the group become known as the 'Repertory Players'. They took up residence in a room above Webberley's bookshop in Hanley which could hold 100 audience members. After several years, the group sought new premises.

In 1933 the group took a three year lease from the church council on the former church of St. Simon and St. Jude in Beresford Street, Shelton, originally opened as a mission church in 1879. It took three months to convert the church into a fully-functioning theatre.

A stage was constructed, 40ft wide and 23ft deep, with a scene dock to hold three sets. Dressing rooms were provided along with a small kitchen to provide a buffet for the interval. 250 tip-up seats were installed on a raked floor facing the stage and the windows were blacked out. The church roof was left and was said to give a "picturesque half-timbered effect". Being a converted church the front-of-house facilities were negligible with the main entrance leading almost straight into the auditorium[375].

The opening production was 'Lean Harvest' by Ronald Jeans, directed by Laurence Steele. All manner of plays were presented by the Repertory Players over the years, including 'The Admiral Crichton' by J.M. Barrie (1934), 'An Inspector Calls' by J.B. Priestley (1952), 'The Glass Menagerie' by Tennessee Williams (1966) and 'Toad of Toad Hall' (1984). Even musicals were presented in the small space, particularly the operettas of Gilbert and Sullivan.

The group had outgrown the increasingly dilapidated site by the 1990s, and a move to the empty Empire Theatre in Longton was planned. Paperwork was waiting to be signed until disaster struck and their new home was destroyed by fire on New Years Eve 1992. The Rep abandoned their plans to move and instead looked towards constructing a purpose-built theatre. The site chosen was in Leek Road and operations moved to the new theatre in 1997.

The former Rep building still stands on College Road, Stoke.

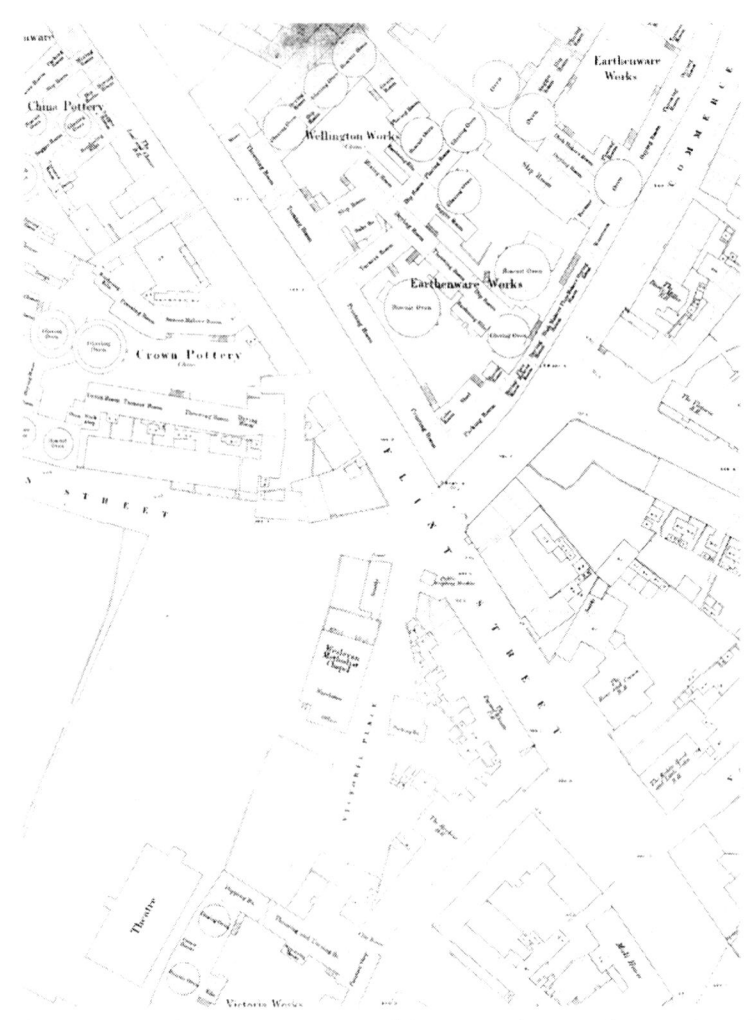

Above. 1855 Ordnance Survey map of Longton, showing the junction of Commerce Street, The Strand (then Flint Street) and Clayton Street. The Royal Alma Theatre can be seen bottom left in Clayton Place, off Clayton Street.

Royal Alma Theatre, Longton

The Royal Alma Theatre stood in Clayton Place, off Clayton Street in Longton, and was opened by Matthew Wardhaugh.

Born in London in 1813, Wardhaugh was orphaned at a young age and began his employment backstage at the Theatre Royal Drury Lane. He later became a travelling actor touring around the country, particularly northern towns. When visiting Longton he pitched his touring cart at Berry Bank and was said to do "a good business in Lane End".

Eventually Wardhaugh built his first permanent theatre in Longton, a structure of wood located in Clayton Square, Longton, measuring 105ft by 50ft in size[376].

This 'Royal Alma Theatre', named after a recent battle in the Crimea, opened on 11th November 1854 with the play 'Morna the Forsaken'[377]. The following week, beginning 18th November, 'The Will and the Way; Or The Mysteries of Carrow Abbey' was presented. The following year in Spring 1855, the residents of Longton could have seen Herr Schmidt, the 'Strongest Man in the World.', 'The Egyptian Fire-Worshippers' and 'The Sicilian Pirate'. Boxes were charged at 1s, the gallery 3d and the pit 6d[378].

During the successful license renewal at the Petty Sessions in Newcastle in 1860 the awarding magistrates said that they believed that the theatre "was conducted with great propriety."[379]

Wardhaugh operated from the building, along with his other three wooden theatres in Bury, Barnsley and Leigh until the opening of his new Royal Victoria Theatre in Longton in 1868, just a short walk from the Royal Alma. The Royal Alma had been dismantled by 1878[380].

Above. Poster for a 'Comic Pantomime' at the Royal Victoria Theatre in 1870. Taken from Farmer's Borough Almanck.

Royal Victoria Theatre, Longton

The Royal Victoria Theatre was opened in Berry Lane, Longton, near to the site where owner Matthew Wardhaugh had pitched his travelling theatre many years previously. Prior to construction of the Royal Victoria, Wardhaugh had been based at the Royal Alma Theatre, off Clayton Street.

The new building was designed by James Rigby and constructed in brick by local builder Gregory Spicer[381]. Seating around 1,800, the building measured 100 ft by 51ft with a raked pit and gallery[382]. Boxes were installed above the gallery, fitted with carpet and chairs[383]. A stone bust of Shakespeare formed part of the internal decoration of the building, surrounded by portraits of famed persons of the theatre world including Mrs. Siddons, John Kemble, Handel, Purcell and Sheridan. The front of the circle was decorated with images from various Shakespeare plays, all painted by resident artist Frank Briggs[384].

On opening night, Saturday 11th January 1868, the plays 'The Minute-Gun at Sea', and 'The Dead Shot' were presented, featuring London actors William Henry Morton and Annie Powell. From the stage, Matthew Wardhaugh gave a speech thanking the Mayor and Borough Magistrates for granting him his first license in the town. Prices were 6d in the pit stalls, 3d in the gallery, and 2s for a box. It was advertised as "the most beautiful temple of the Drama within thirty miles", not that there was much competition at that time.

In an attempt to compete with the new Royal Victoria, the Royal Pottery Theatre in Hanley staged "the best pantomime every produced in the Potteries" in this opening week, and organised a special direct train between the two towns.

In the first month after opening, Wardhaugh staged 'Sweeny Todd', 'Bleeding Nun', 'Wild Meg of the Hills' and 'Hamlet'; he was known to be a great lover of Shakespeare. Wardhaugh eventually closed his other theatres and settled in Longton, becoming mayor in 1883[385]. Wardhaugh made the theatre available to present a series of operas in order to raise money for the Longton Atheneaum, but these failed to make profit[386].

Wardhaugh passed away on 27th March 1888, but had previously let and then sold the building to Wallace Revill. He subsequently sold the theatre to the Longton and District Theatre Company, who were constructing the new Queen's Theatre adjacent to the site. Revill made a large profit in the process[387].

James Elphinstone Jnr. became manager on 4th June 1888 on behalf of the new owners. By this point the theatre was known as the 'Theatre Royal and Opera House'. In the week of 3rd September 1888, the final week before the new Queen's opened, J. H. Cyndee appeared in 'Hamlet', 'Belphegor', and 'Ticket-of-Leave Man' at the Theatre Royal.

The Theatre Royal's dramatic license was transferred over to the new Queen's upon its opening[388]. Elphinstone continued to offer the old venue after this for "non-dramatic companies, concerts and entertainments"[389], having obtained a license for "music, singing and dancing" from the Borough Police Court[390]. Over Christmas that year Professor E. K. Crocker was engaged with his famous educated horses, the "best schooled and best educated horses in the world."[391] It was then advertised as the 'Old Theatre Royal, Longton'.

In 1890, mayor John Aynsley presided over a political meeting at the Victoria Theatre in favour of the Unionist candidate W. S. Allen[392]. It was reported to still be operating as a theatre in 1892 but surely closed shortly after[393]. The building was subsequently put up for auction by the Longton and District Theatre Company, along with the fire-damaged Queen's Theatre. The sale was held at the Crown and Anchor Hotel on 12th June 1895, where it was advertised as covering 850 square yards and having no internal fittings. It sold for £550[394].

The building later became the armoury and drill hall to the 'A' company of the 1st Volunteer Battalion of the North Staffordshire Regiment, led in 1904 by Captain George A. Mitcheson[395].

By the late 1940s the former theatre was being used by the firm of James Davies Ltd. to produce ceramics transfers. On 6th May 1949 the building was gutted by a huge fire, with flames leaping up 100ft into the Longton skies. Machines were drafted in from Longton, Burslem and Tunstall and one fireman closely escaped death as the bust of Shakespeare fell from the building. Another two firemen were injured. Structural damage meant that the walls had to be demolished down to the first floor level for safety.

At the time, the company were in the process of constructing a new building facing Stafford Street (now The Strand), development of which

Old Theatres in the Potteries

led to the rebuilding of the theatre site on the same footprint after the fire, with the Shakespeare bust installed on the outside of the building overlooking Berry Lane[396].

The late eighties saw the front part of this building occupied by Jomen's, a clothing store[397]. This was demolished in the early 1990s as part of redevelopment efforts in the area by iM Properties. The bust of Shakespeare was thought at the time to have been saved. Witnesses saw its removal on an elevated platform however the whereabouts of the bust are currently unknown, and it is not held in the collections of the Potteries Museum.

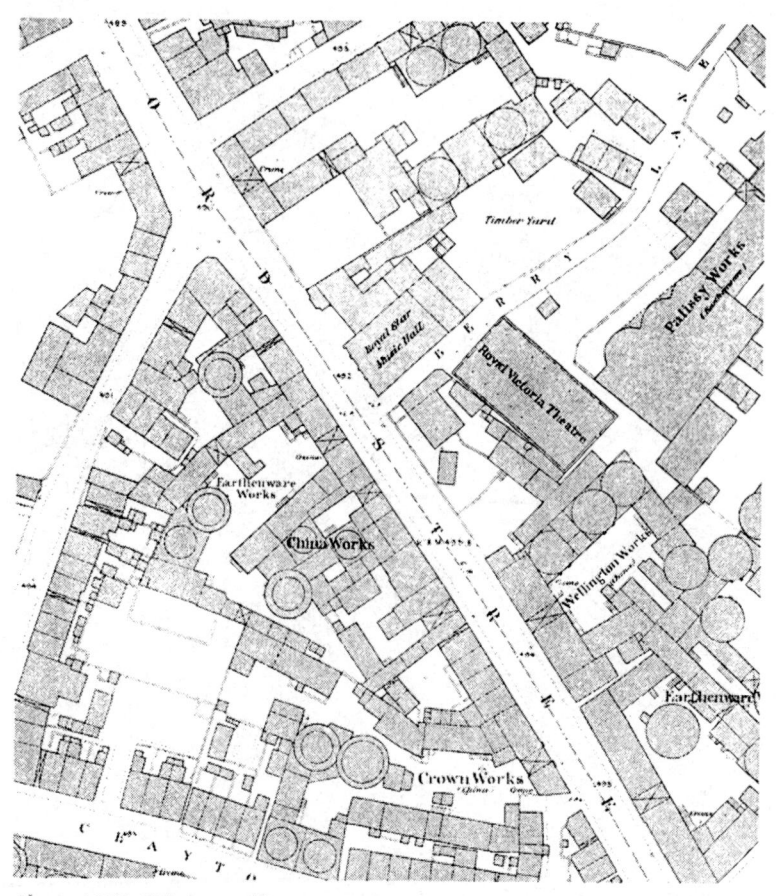

Above. 1878 OS map of Longton, showing the Royal Victoria Theatre on Berry Lane, off Stafford Street.

141

Old Theatres in the Potteries

Queen's Theatre, Longton

The Queens Theatre was at least the third theatre in Longton, following the Royal Alma and Royal Victoria. Work began in January 1888 on behalf of the Longton and District Theatre Company, directors of which included mayor and businessman John Aynsley, Dr. William Dawes, Hampton Waters, Henry Hill, A. E. Walters, George Charles Kent and David Chapman[398].

The theatre was designed by local architect John Taylor and construction was carried out by Tom S. Bromage of Longton. The location chosen was on the corner of Commerce Street and Chancery Lane, formerly the site of pottery works. The building would be named the 'Queen's Theatre', chosen as Queen Victoria had celebrated her Golden Jubilee in 1887. The nearby Queen's Park also derived its name in this manner.

The main entrance on Commerce Street was built of red stone in the free renaissance style. It was built with three storeys, with a projecting left-hand bay with an arched window above the main entrance. The rest of the frontage to the right contained three sets of windows above three shops on the ground floor, which were to be let to provide additional income.

The stalls could hold 640 persons; with the first two rows comprising of upholstered seats and the rest of wooden benches. The dress circle could hold 191; the front two rows being fitted with velvet tip-up chairs, with an upper circle holding 250 to the rear of the dress on the same level. Six private boxes were also installed holding 40 in total, and the gallery could accommodate another 454, a total of 1,575. The venue was advertised as having a capacity of 3,400 however; the rest presumably coming from standing capacity[399]. The balconies were supported with iron columns and access was gained from the entrances in Commerce Street, which led via a stairwell almost directly into the auditorium.

Stage-wise, the dimensions were 63ft wide and 48ft deep, with three bridges, a vampire trap and two diving traps built in. The installation of the stage was supervised by John Turner of the Grand Theatre, Leeds. The proscenium arch was 27ft wide and 34ft 6in tall, and decorated with moulded plasterwork by George Jackson and Sons of London. The total construction cost was contracted as being £12,000.

AUTHORISED PROGRAMME OF

Queen's Theatre,
LONGTON.

Sole Lessee & Manager, Mr. J. Elphinstone, jun.

Monday, September 10,

ROLLO BALMAIN'S Co.

IN

HOODMAN
BLIND.

From the Princess Theatre, London.

New and Beautiful Scenery by Mr. William Quick; Properties modelled and designed by Mr Chris McQuire; Mechanical Effects by Messrs H Cross and H Boothroyd; Limelight and Gas Effects by Robert Rose and J Harrison; Musical Director, Mr. R. Watson.

Above. Extract from front cover of the first week's programme for the Queen's Theatre, Longton, from 10th September 1888. The opening night's programme was printed in gold lettering.

Old Theatres in the Potteries

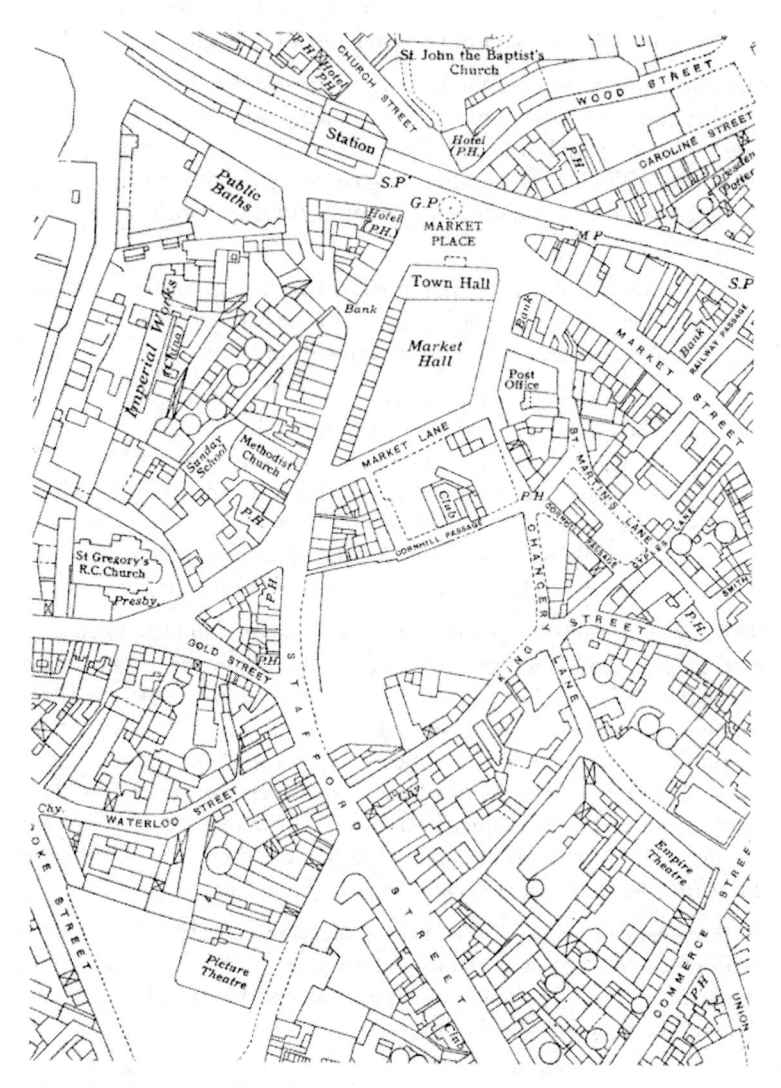

Above. 1930s Ordnance Survey Map of Longton, showing the Empire Theatre at the junction of Chancery Lane and Commerce Street. The shell of the Royal Victoria Theatre can also be seen.

145

Construction began in January 1888 and was still in progress at the time of opening[400]. The first lessee was James Elphinstone Jnr., proprietor of the neighbouring Theatre Royal, Longton, and son of the proprietor of the Theatre Royal, Hanley[401]. He took a twenty-one year lease on the venue; starting at £850 for one year before rising to £900 annually.

Opening night came on Monday 10th September 1888. At 7.30pm the opening ceremony was performed by company director and mayor John Aynsley before a packed house of over 3,000. Before the performance of 'Hoodman's Blind', leader of the acting company Rollo Balmain appeared on stage to recite an original prologue to the occasion which included the lines:

> "Why I am here, dear friends, before this curtain
> May seem to you, perhaps, somewhat uncertain
> You've come, I know, to see and hear the play!"
>
> "In this new house will be, you will, I'm sure, agree
> Theres some indebtedness to John Aynsley,
> Also to Taylor, the architect, for his structural skill,
> And Bromage the builder, who has worked with a will.
> They say the mummer's lot the chief of lotteries,
> Prove you to Elphinstone, 'tis not so in the Potteries"

The Stage commented that the performance "went without a hitch from first to last" and that the opening "could hardly have been more auspicious"[402]. No review of the evening's production was printed in the *Staffordshire Sentinel*, "owing to want of foresight of the part of the management" to send them free tickets, a luxury which was afforded to competing paper *The Staffordshire Knot*. The tickets would have cost 2s 6d in the Dress Circle, 2s in the orchestra stalls, 1s in the upper circle, 6d in the pit, and 3d in the gallery. A private box could be reserved for either £1 1s (to hold four), £2 2s (to hold six) or £3 3s (to hold eight).

By arrangement with W. D. Philips, general manager of the North Staffordshire Railway, a special late train was run to Blythe Bridge leaving Longton at 11pm. The following week, Waldon's Original Co. presented 'Fun on the Bristol' at the theatre.

For the first christmas of the theatre, a large spectacle was produced entitled 'Forward to the Front'. It featured over 250 people on the stage including a grand march past by soldiers, sailors and marines, with "new and magnificent scenery", all at normal prices[403].

In an effort to attract visitors from the other pottery towns and beyond, tickets for the dress circle and boxes started to be sold at half price to those travelling from towns other than Longton, providing they possessed a valid rail ticket[404].

Following the Mossfield Colliery disaster in 1889, Elphinstone offered the theatre for a sacred concert, with the Carl Rosa opera company providing their services for free. The concert took place on Sunday 27th October 1889 and raised £80 19s 3d for the relief fund[405].

James Elphinstone Jnr. soon ran into financial trouble. He was sued by Rimma and Leuze, opera managers, for their share of the receipts at the theatre, amounting to £35 2s. 2d. Elphinstone resorted to name-calling in court, saying the pair ran "the worst opera company that ever appeared in Longton". The judge found in favour of the plaintiffs and Elphinstone was forced to pay £70 in expenses.

The case contributed to Elphinstone's bankruptcy and a meeting of his creditors was held at the North Stafford Hotel on Wednesday 12th March 1890. In total, 108 creditors were owed £3,357. His father James H. Elphinstone was the largest, being owed £1,300 for cash and cheque advances. After liquidation, the assets would not pay off the total of the preferred creditors, amounting to £649 17s. 9 ½d. He stated that it was the high rents at the theatre, £900 a year, that were his downfall. His brother Charles backed him up, saying that he believed the theatre was not even worth £500 per year[406].

Actor Edmund Tearle took over the theatre and commenced a renovation project. The circle was walled in and boxes enlarged, as were the refreshment rooms. Draughts into the auditorium were also eliminated using folding gates and heating apparatus. The theatre was redecorated throughout in the Louis XIV style with the "best known London artists" employed to carry out the work. The proscenium was painted and gilded, the ceiling painted to become "a work of art" and claret coloured drapery fitted throughout. The work was carried out by Peter Bennion of Longton to designs from the original architect John Taylor at a cost of £3,000[407].

It reopened on 15th September 1890 with a production of Sheridan Knowles' tragedy of 'Virginius', starring Tearle in the title role. Sir Henry Irving, Mrs. Langtry, and Richard D'Oyly Carte sent telegrams of congratulations for the opening night[408]. Tearle's tenancy ended in March 1893[409] and the operation of the theatre was continued by the directors of the company, under the management of its secretary A. S Walters[410]. It reopened for Easter week with the pantomime "Little Jack Horner" after a week of refurbishment.

On 28th September 1894 the theatre succumbed to what was said at the time to be "one of the most alarming and destructive fires which has ever occurred in Longton." At 6.50am, passerby Charles Pedley spotted smoke pouring from the building. The fire brigade were alerted and proceeded to Commerce Street with the new steam-powered fire engine recently acquired by the corporation. Due to the inflammable nature of the materials inside, the fire spread with great speed and one by one, the tiers collapsed inside the auditorium. Just before eight'o clock the roof came down, followed by an explosion as the gas lines erupted. The force of this seriously damaged the theatre and blew out the windows in the facade. It was felt by people living five miles away and blew over those in the street below. By the time further engines arrived from Stoke and Hanley the auditorium was destroyed and efforts were directed towards saving the frontage and shops below, and also to prevent the flames from spreading to neighbouring properties. It took six hours to bring the fire under control and the damage was estimated at over £17,000. The auditorium was totally destroyed except for the exterior walls and stage opening. Fortunately the stone facade, including the three shops, offices and entrance vestibule were saved[411].

At a meeting on the 1st October the directors unanimously voted to rebuild the theatre as soon as possible, despite the building being underinsured for just one third of its value[412]. They also gifted ten guineas to the company of 'Uncle Tom's Cabin' who were playing at the theatre on night of the fire and lost nearly all of their scenery and effects. Benefit concerts were also held in Longton Town Hall for the visiting company.

By December 1894 reconstruction work had begun. Frank Matcham was engaged as architect to construct a theatre to hold 2,400 housed in the shell of the old and retaining the John Taylor frontage. Fifty tons of collapsed metal work were removed, and work was expected to be complete by Easter[413]. During the work, one of the remaining walls was brought down during a storm in December 1894.

The work had ground to a halt by the following June, with the rebuilding by the firm of Inskips and Sons said to have progressed "tardily".

The Longton and District Theatre Company decided to sell the site as was in an auction at the Crown and Anchor Hotel on 12th June, along with the shell of the neighbouring Royal Victoria. The lot was for the

> "block at corner of Commerce Street and Chancery Lane, along with three lockup shops and office over. Cleared after fire, roof nearly completed. Immediately restoration."

Only one bid of £2000 was made, and the lot subsequently withdrawn[414]. Work soon restarted, this time at the hands of builder Peter Bennion[415] and was progressing "speedily" by February 1896[416].

Described as "one of the most handsome in the provinces", little structural alteration was made to the principal entrance in Commerce Street, and the three shops were still present in the facade. Redecoration took place internally however, with raised leather paper on the walls and a new ornamental front to the pay office. From here access was provided to the dress circle, upper circle and stalls, whilst entrance to the pit and gallery was from Chancery Lane. Crush-rooms, saloons, smoking rooms and retiring rooms were provided for the patrons on all the levels.

Around 2,800 persons could be accommodated over the stalls, two circles, gallery, and boxes[417]. The sight lines from the circles were said to "perfect" due to the absence of support columns afforded by the cantilevered balconies. Ample exits were provided, fitted with Briggs' patent panic bolts[418]. The auditorium was decorated on an "elaborate" scale, with moulded plasterwork installed on the fronts of the balconies and ceiling[419]. Decoration was by Binns of Halifax, with draperies along with the carpets and seating in shades of pink terracotta.

The stage was enormous, measuring 64ft wide by 57ft deep with a 31ft proscenium opening. An iron and asbestos fireproof curtain was built in and for added safety from fire, electric light was fitted throughout, powered by a 23 horsepower gas dynamo beneath the stage. A 22ft deep pit was in place beneath the stage providing storage for scenery. Provision was also made for scenery to be flown up into the fly tower[420]. Store and property rooms were housed backstage, with large and well-ventilated dressing rooms located beneath the auditorium, equipped with hot and cold running water.

Following the award of a dramatic licence by the Longton Stipendiary Court[421], the theatre opened on Wednesday 18th May 1896 with Mrs. Fortescue and her company in 'Pygmalion and Galatea'. Opening night saw a gigantic crowd form in Commerce Street, so large that police were employed to clear a path for arriving carriages[422]. The unveiling of the drop cloth, which depicted Trentham Hall, caused a large outbreak of applause, as did the fading up of the electric lights, which still seemed like a novelty to the people of Longton in 1896. Director David Chapman addressed the audience to officially open the theatre, before all those assembled joined with orchestra leader Guillaume Leone in singing the national anthem. The opening performance of 'Pygmalion and Galatea' was said to be "very ably performed" by the company.

The Duchess of Sutherland hired the theatre on Tuesday 8th November 1904 in order to present a charitable performance in aid of the Society for the Prevention of Cruelty to Children. The Duchess, along with Lady Lathom, sat in a private box adorned with fresh flowers to watch the production of 'His Excellency the Governor', a farcical romance set on an island of the empire. The amateur cast included a number of the Duchess' friends including Colonel Newnham-Davis, The Honourable W. Goschen and Colonel Cotton-Jodrell. The *Staffordshire Sentinel* reviewed the play, describing it as "acted to perfection."[423]

The theatre continued to present a mix of drama, comedy, operetta and opera, including appearances from J.W. Turner's English Opera Company, 'The Gay Gordons', LeRoy, Talma and Bosco in 'Lady Kinton's Necklace' and 'The Dandy Doctor' with Edward Marris. The theatre was even used by the Dresden Amateur Operatic Society in February 1911 for their production of 'Ermine'[424].

The large stage and backstage facilities meant that animals could easily be accommodated. The large scene store beneath the stage was said to be used for stabling various circus animals for shows. The play 'The Fiends of London' was staged in April 1904 featuring live horses on stage as part of the action, the subject of the play being the Grand National[425].

Old Theatres in the Potteries

Queen's Theatre,
LONGTON. Telephone: Longton 57.

Proprietors . . . . . The New Longton Theatre Ltd.
General Manager . . . . . Mr. H. Sherriff Howard

Wednesday, Thursday, Friday, and Saturday,
FEBRUARY 22nd, 23rd, 24th, and 25th, 1911.
FOUR NIGHTS ONLY, THE
Dresden Amateur Operatic Society
Will Present (by Arrangement with JOSEPH WILLIAMS, Ltd.) the Popular and Delightful COMIC OPERA—
ERMINIE.
IN AID OF LOCAL CHARITIES.

PROGRAMME FOR THIS EVENING.

Prices of Admission during this Engagement.

Dress Circle & Stalls	Upper Circle & Pit Stalls	Pit	Gallery
2s. 6d.	1s.	6d.	4d.

EARLY DOORS to Pit Stalls, 6d.   Upper Circle, 3d.   Pit, 2d. Extra.
Early Doors Open at 6.30.   Ordinary Doors Open at 7.0.   Commence at 7.30.
Children in arms not admitted.   Seats not Guaranteed unless previously Booked.   No Money returned.
Smoking strictly prohibited

Box PLAN may be seen and Seats booked at the Theatre daily from 11 to 3, or during the performance. Letters and Telegrams addressed Box Office will receive prompt attention.   No Booking Fees.   Telephone Longton 57.

Musical Director . . Mr. FRANK HUGHES | Engineer . . . Mr. W. OWEN
Master Carpenter . . Mr. H. DUVAL | Bill Inspector . . Mr. E. ASPAIN

Late Trains for Fenton, Stoke, Newcastle, Etruria, Hanley, Burslem, Tunstall, Longport, Alsager and Crewe, every Evening at 10-33.
For all Stations to Uttoxeter, 11-14, Mond ys and Saturdays only.
For Trentham, Barlaston, and Stone, Mondays, Thursdays & Saturdays at 10-56.
For all Stations to Leek (except Fenton Manor), Thursdays & Saturdays at 10-33.
TRAMCARS to Stoke, Dresden and the Meir after the Performance.
N.B. The Theatre Cars will run to Denbigh Castle, Stoke, each evening.

The Refreshment Saloons are under the direct control of the Management and everything will be found of the very best Quality.

Tradesmen are requested not to supply Goods to the Theatre without a Printed Order signed by the Manager.

NOTE.—The Carpets, Seating and Upholstery in this Theatre are cleaned by the "Aspirator" Air Suction Cleaning Machine. Can be seen in operation any time by appointment. Full particulars from BAWICK & Co., 3, Stone Road, Longton.

W. H. Wright, High Street Printing Works, Longton.

Above. Front cover of a programme for the Dresden Amateur Operatic Society's production of Ermine at the Queen's in February 1911.

151

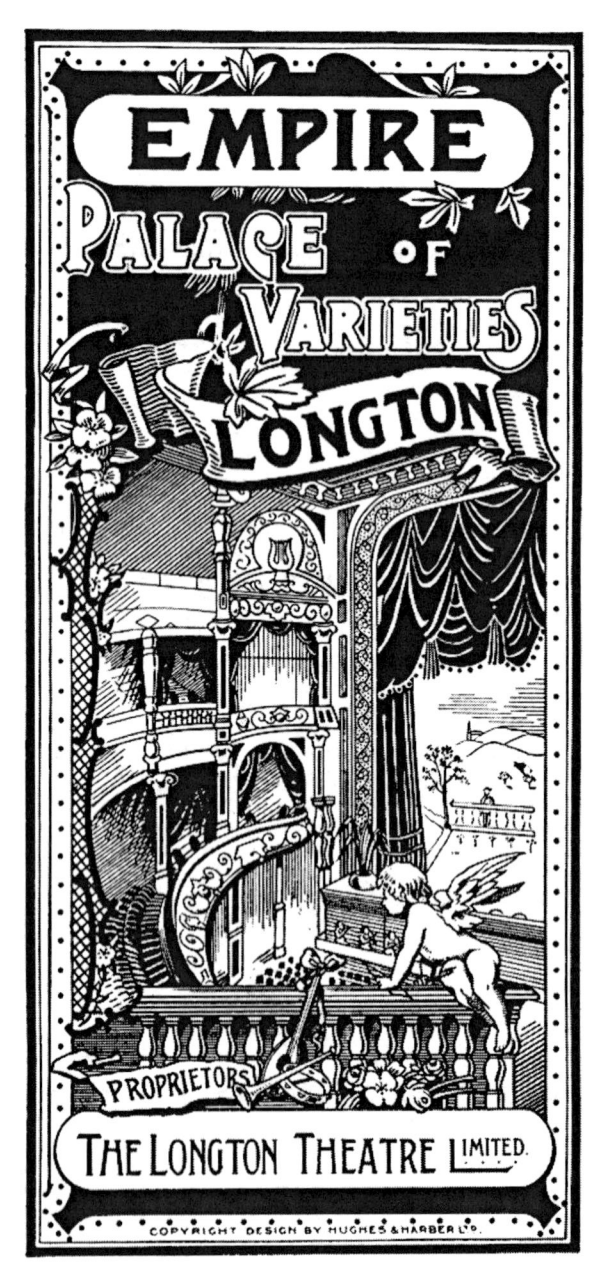

Above. Front cover of a 1915 programme for the renamed 'Empire'.

The Queen's came under new management in 1914 and in the new, patriotic spirit brought about by the outbreak of war was renamed the 'Empire Palace of Varieties'. It was also accompanied by a change in the type of show presented, becoming a variety theatre in the style of a music hall. After redecoration it reopened on Monday 3rd August 1914 for Wakes week with a line up of "high class" attractions. Tom E. Finglass the "cowboy coon" headed the bill, with support from Austen Temple the magician, Jack Warner the patter comedian, singer Edna Clyde and George Marriott's company in the comedy 'Shoemaker's Luck'. The eight Empire Girls, a "novel singing and dancing act" were advertised to appear however the trunk carrying their costumes went astray during transit on the wartime railway network[426].

The Empire was sold again in 1917 to a new group headed by G. E. Williams, formerly of Moss Empires, and in a short space of time the theatre was totally refurbished. The auditorium was repainted in shades of gold and blue with new complementary carpet and wallpaper. Tapestry panels were fitted along the side walls and gold velvet seats fitted throughout. Front-of-house was also redecorated with oriental wallpapers and new stage scenery was also installed. The management assured the public that they would "secure nothing but first-class attractions". The Empire reopened on Monday 24th December 1917 with a production of 'High Explosives - A Musical Revusical Exhilarator'.

The increasing popularity of cinema meant that the Empire was losing business, especially with competition from four cinemas within walking distance of the theatre. The theatre was sold at auction on 9th November 1921 at the North Stafford Hotel[427].

William Hall and Norman Edwards were directors of the new company. Following a christmas engagement of the pantomime 'Beauty and the Beast', the Empire closed on New Years Eve 1921 for reconstruction and the installation of projection equipment. It reopened on Monday 23rd January 1922 as a cinema, with variety acts still appearing between the pictures. Upon reopening, Harry Grice was manager, previously holding the role at the nearby Alexandra Palace. That week, the main attraction was the film 'Peck's Bad Boy' starring Jackie Coogan, with live acts from Will Van Allen "Famous Musical Tramp Comedian" and Ernest Mitchell "Popular Baritone"[428].

Above. Postcard showing the frontage of the Empire Theatre, c. 1921. Note the two men standing on the roof.

Old Theatres in the Potteries

EMPIRE - Longton

MONDAY, MAY 22nd AND DURING WEEK.
6-40 ——————— TWICE NIGHTLY ——————— 8-50

The Biggest All Star Bill Seen Here!

The talk of New York—Chicago and San Francisco—

THE GREAT
RADIANA

The most sensational Electrical Novelty in the World.

BOOT & BOLON	A NOVEL ATTRACTION! MYSTERY GIFTS
MATINEE THURS., AT 2-30.	SOMETHING FOR NOTHING! GIVEN AWAY AT EVERY PERFORMANCE.
Mdlle. HELENE	Bring Some Unusual Article with you. . You may be asked for anything from a Safety Pin to a Kitchen Stove
VARDEL FOUR	
Dale, Dale & Dale	DON'T FORGET TO COME PREPARED TO RECEIVE A FREE GIFT FROM—
TOMMY TRINDER	RADIANA
JEN LATONA	Our Crazy Gang

DO NOT MISS THIS BIG ATTRACTION!!

Taylors Theatrical Printers, Wombwell, Yorks.

Above. Flyer for week beginning 22nd May 1933, with a variety bill including Tommy Trinder and 'Radiana', the magical box.

Full stage shows still took place; just five weeks after opening as a cinema the christmas pantomime made a return visit. The stage was still in use in the thirties, an example being in May 1933 when "The Great Radiana, the most sensational Electrical Novelty in the world" topped the variety bill. Lower down the bill was a young Tommy Trinder, later to present 'Sunday Night at the London Palladium'. Later that year, Pierce and Rosslyn and Wal Langry appeared in an "All Star Vaudeville Bill"[429].

Over the years, the Empire gained a reputation as having its own resident spook, reportedly seen stalking the second balcony. Nicknamed 'Charlie', local legend paints several stories. He was either a circus performer who died attempting to catch a bullet between his teeth on stage, a distraught widower who leapt to his death from the 'gods'[430] or a member of staff who fell from the top balcony and broke his neck[431]. Perhaps Charlie was not one ghost, but three...

Part of the Derwent circuit, the cinema was acquired by the ABC group in the early thirties. They commissioned a major renovation in 1952 where the sound equipment was upgraded and parts of the interior remodelled, straightening out many of the winding Victorian corridors. The interior was also redecorated, reseated and re-carpeted[432]. The facade also saw extensive works. It was reopened on Monday 28th July 1952 by the Deputy Lord Mayor and Lady Mayoress and Alderman Mrs. Horace Barks. Film star Richard Todd was also in attendance at the event, where the John Wayne film 'The Quiet Man' was shown. At some point following this the top floors of the facade were removed, giving it a squatter, squarer appearance.

Unable to compete with television, the Empire closed as a cinema on 2nd April 1966 with a showing of Elvis Presley in 'Harem Holiday'. As with many old theatres the building gave itself over to bingo, operating as the Tudor Bingo Club and then as Coral Bingo.

As part of the City Architect's 1966 report into a 'civic theatre' in the city, the building was investigated for conversion. Unlike his poor opinion of Hanley's Theatre Royal, the City Architect was most favourable to the Empire. The location was praised for being located next to the new Longton Bus Station, and front of house was more than adequate at all levels. The auditorium's curved design was said to give a level of intimacy, even at the second tier, and provided "excellent" acoustics. He did state that the top level would have some sightline issues, however this had already been closed off for several years.

The huge stage, larger than all but three of the West End theatres, could accommodate any show and could even be converted into housing a 'theatre-in-the-round', having a larger footprint in itself than the whole of the Victoria Theatre in Hartshill. New stage equipment would be needed however if the conversion took place, due to the age and lack of use of that in place. The large number of store rooms backstage and beneath would also meet any needs that a production would require. Other work needed would be the installation of an orchestra pit, lost over its years as a cinema, and improvement of fire proofing throughout. The Cultural Activities sub-committee chose not to pursue the conversion and the Empire remained as a bingo hall[433]. A false ceiling was installed at some point between the first and second circle, and the building was made a listed building in 1977[434].

As the original auditorium decoration was relatively unaltered during its bingo career, it led theatre historian Christopher Brereton to write of the venue in 1982:

> "marvellous...one of the best and least-known examples of Frank Matcham's surviving works"[435]

The bingo operation closed in 1991 and the building put up for sale for £175,000[436], featuring on the local television news to drum up business.

Towards the end of 1992 the local Repertory Theatre had agreed to purchase the theatre and spend £750,000 on a refurbishment project, turning it into "a receiving house for professional touring groups" as well as functioning as their new base[437]. The appropriate papers were set to the signed at the beginning of 1993.

Above. The facade of the Empire in January 1993, following the fire. Scaffolding was quickly erected to make the facade safe.

Above. The side wall of the auditorium facing Chancery Lane in the process of demolition. January 1993. Longton Bus Station can be seen far right.

Old Theatres in the Potteries

Above. The rear of the Empire during demolition, most of the auditorium has already gone. In the background can be seen the Commerce Street works, originally home to Chetham and Woolley in 1796.

Above. The former site of the Empire Theatre, now a council car park.

On the evening of New Years Eve 1992, BBC Radio Stoke announced that a large building in Commerce Street was on fire. Once again, the Empire was ablaze in what was said by the Chief Fire Officer to be "one of the most serious fires in the county for many years". The fire spread throughout the entire theatre from basement to roof, with flames leaping high into the Longton sky. The surrounding pavements were raised by the heat of the fire and littered with burning debris, raining down from the sky[438].

New Year's partygoers at the neighbouring Leisurebowl and Maina Mapi restaurant were evacuated, whilst many more came to watch the spectacle from outside the telephone exchange opposite. It took 100 firefighters four hours to bring the fire under control, and days for it to be totally extinguished. Investigators believed that the fire was started by "trespassers".

Longton Chamber of Trade chairman Ellis Bevan demanded a public enquiry into the fire and launched a campaign to save the remains of the theatre. Sadly it was not to be and following a meeting of English Heritage, owners of the site Bass Breweries, and the City Council, demolition of the stage and auditorium walls began on the 5th of January.

The remains were later purchased by iM Properties who were at the time redeveloping the Bennett Precinct area of the town. The facade was surrounded by scaffolding as piece by piece, the remains were declared unsafe and parts removed and put into storage[439].

Finally, just the ground floor of the facade stood and after gaining permission from Environment Secretary John Gummer, the remains were completely demolished early in 1997[440]. The stored remains were delisted in September 1998[441], their current location unknown. The corner of Commerce Street and Chancery Lane now is the site of a council car park.

Panopticon Theatre, Longton

The Panopticon Theatre, Longton, was located on Edensor Road. It began life as a skating rink in the latter part of the 1900s before becoming the Panopticon in 1911. Not strictly a theatre, it presented a series of short, silent films linked together by vaudeville acts, an amalgamation termed 'cine-variety'. The building could seat around 2,000 and was fitted with a stage 36ft wide and 12ft deep. Three dressing rooms were also provided[442].

Monday 3rd April 1911 saw Carl Howlett's Royal Marionettes, Muriel Vivian - comedienne and dancer, and Barry Moon - the descriptive vocalist linking a series of "the finest pictures in the Potteries"[443]. It was renamed later that year to the 'Alexandra Palace'. In 1912 the early colour process 'Kinemacolor' was exhibited here, requiring planning permission from the council to alter the building[444].

It became part of the ABC group for a period in the thirties before passing into private hands. It closed in August 1957, subsequently housing bingo and shops. The building became Shelley's Laserdome by the late eighties, a popular rave venue owned by John Matthews. It gained an association with drug dealing leading the police, city council and magistrates to close down the venue. The building was demolished in May 1994 to make way for the A50 relief road through the town[445].

Old Theatres in the Potteries

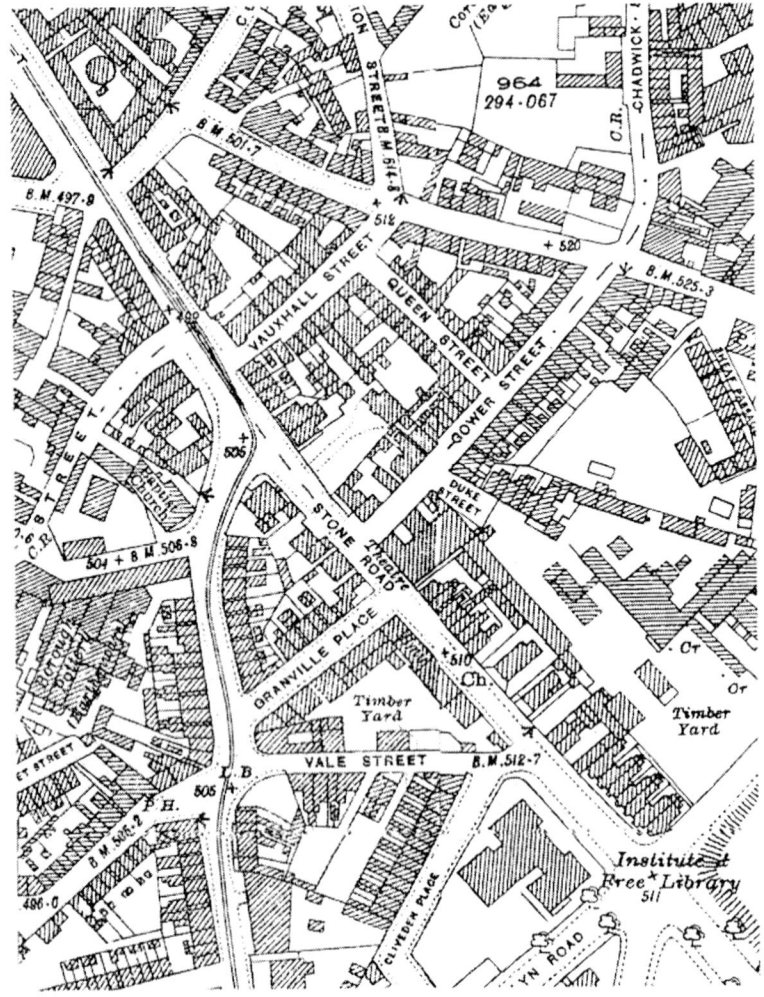

Above. 1924 Ordnance Survey map of Longton, showing the Regent Theatre on Stone Road in the centre. The Sutherland Institute, now housing Longton Library, can be seen bottom right. Most of this area has been lost with the construction of the new A50.

Regent Theatre, Longton

The Regent Theatre, Longton was located at the junction of Gower Street and Stone Road, Longton (now Lightwood Road).

The building was originally opened as a cinema in 1909 called the 'Picturedrome', a silent cinema with vaudeville acts playing onstage between the films. The building could seat 480 and was constructed mostly of timber[446].

Monday 3rd April 1911 saw Ella Blair - the New York Clipper, and Mark Merry -"Quaint Comedian" on the bill, in between the star pictures of 'Arsene Lupine' and 'The Oath and the Man'[447].

In 1921 the Picturedrome became the 'Regent Theatre', presenting mostly a programme of variety[448]. 1935 saw Rex Deering compering "The Big Idea – an all-laughter, high-speed presentation". Acts including comedian Billy May, soubrette and toe tapper Marjorie Bennett, staircase dancer Lew Freeman, and The Deviants, "variety's most versatile musical offering", all at bargain prices starting at 4d. In 1936 the building was closed down on safety grounds, said to be unsafe for the public. Sometime later, the building was demolished.

The area where the building stood was destroyed during construction of the A50 in the early 1990s, and would have been located just to the south of the bridge joining Lightwood Road to the centre of Longton.

Index

Abberley, John..................................54
ABC Weekend Television. 117, 119, 120
Adams, William...................................7
Adamson, Peter.................................63
Ainsworth, Harrison..........................92
Aldridge, Marion...............................56
Alexandra Music Hall, Hanley............81
Alexandra Palace Cinema, Longton...161
Allen Edwardes, T............................131
Allen, Frank......................................98
Allen, W.S..140
Ambassador Theatre Group......109, 111
Art Business, The.............................108
Arts Council....................................109
Ashford, George................................81
Ayckbourn, Alan..............................117
Aynsley, John................140, 143, 146
Bader, Douglas.................................113
Baggaley, Joseph................................14
Bailey, P...113
Ball, Michael.....................................67
Ball, Steve...25
Balleni, H..77
Balmain, Rollo.................................146
Bamford, ?..31
Barbirolli, John.................................85
Barks, Mr. Horace.............................56
Barks, Mrs. Horace....................56, 156
Barnard, Paul....................................63
Barnes, D..105
Barraclough, Roy.............................118
Barrasford, G.H...............................103
Barry, Arthur....................................15
Bassey, Shirley................................107
Bateman, Samuel..............................42
Batty Harmston, W...........................82
Batty's Circus, Hanley.......................82
BBC Pebble Mill..............................120
Beard, Dorothea...............................45
Beatles, The....................................107
Beatrice, Mademoiselle.....................35
Bennett, Arnold. 14, 102, 105, 119, 120
Bennett, Sir Albert...........................119
Bennion, Peter..........................147, 149
Berry, Arthur............................120, 121
Bert Rigby You're A Fool..................64
Bettany, F..19
Bevan, Ellis.....................................160
Bianci, Morace..................................98
Binns of Halifax..............................149
Biocolor Circuit................................29
Birkett, Arthur...................................45
Birkett, Edmund................................45
Black, Cilla.......................................78
Blobby, Mr..67
Blood Tub...14
Bodley, Edward F..............................73
Booth, General............................12, 82

Bosco, Leotard..................................81
Boswell's Circus..................................82
Boullemier, Anton............................125
Bourne, Hugh...................................118
Bown, B...27
Bracket, Dame Hilda..........................63
Breeze, Jesse.......................................7
Brent, Evelyn...................................107
Briggs, Frank...................................139
Brindley, Joseph..................................7
Brindley, W.......................................19
Broadhurst, H...................................77
Bromage, Tom S..............................143
Bromley, Mr. (Mayor of Hanley) 77
Brook, C. Austin..............................113
Brooke, Gustavus V.......................9, 35
Brooks, Elkie.....................................67
Brooks, Samuel.................................95
Brown, Roy 'Chubby'........................67
Brunton, Mr......................................42
Buccini, Signor..................................97
Bulmar, A..45
Bundred, Thomas..............................31
Burslem Theatres.....................................
    Coliseum......................................27
    Hippodrome............................19, 21
    Lyceum Theatre...........................14
    Poynter's New Theatre.................13
    Queen's Theatre..........................23
    Royal Britannia............................14
    Snape's Theatre...........................14
Cannon and Ball................................67

Capitol Cinema, Hanley....................93
Carl Rosa Opera................................45
Carl Rosa Opera..............................147
Carlton, Arthur R............................123
Casson, Johnny..................................67
Central Hall, Hanley..........................95
Central Lyric Hall, Hanley.................95
Century Theatre, Hanley.................112
Ceramic City Choir...........................85
Chamberlain, J..................................82
Chaplin, Charlie..............................102
Chapman, David......................143, 150
Cheeseman, Joyce............................119
Cheeseman, Peter.....117, 118, 119, 120
Chicago Rock Cafe, Hanley.............104
Chung Ling Soo................................29
Churchill, Tim..................................67
Circus...
    Batty's Circus, Hanley..................82
    Elphinstone's Circus, Hanley........82
    Grand Theatre of Varieties...........97
    Imperial Circus, Hanley................76
    Tontine Street Circus, Hanley.......82
Circus Music Hall, Hanley.................70
City of Stoke-on-Trent Amateur Operatic Society..............................107
Civic Theatre Scheme........................60
Clarke, Arthur...................................56
Clayton, Edward..............................118
Clive, J.H..7
Cole, Nat King..................................85
Coliseum, Burslem............................27

Collins, Lewis	63
Collins, Pat	21, 127
Consolidated Exploration and Finance Company	92
Cooke, George	99
Coonie, Harris	27
Coquelli	29
Cornes and Co. (Builders)	55
Cornes, Cornelius	43
Cotton-Jodrell, Colonel	150
Cotton, Billy	59
Cox, Thomas	7
Crane, H.J.	102
Crichton, Haldane	123
Crocker, Professor	140
Crown Theatre, Stoke	123
Cueette, Cissie	29
Cultural Quarter	108
Cyndee, J.H.	140
D'Oyle Carte Opera	45
D'Oyly Carte, Richard	148
Damaged Lives	29
Davidson, Jim	67
Davies, Alan	67
Dawes, Dr. William	143
Day, Samuel Philips	31
Deacon, Charles	62, 64
Dean, Moya	15
Deering, Rex	163
Dempsey-Ackyroyd Trio	27
Dempsey, Margaret	27
Derbyshire, Eileen	112
Desaris, Monsieur	33
Devonshire, G.T.	45
Dodd, Ken	61, 67
Dow, Mark	77
Drinkwater, Carol	118
Driver, Betty	51
Dudman Bromwich, Mr. and Mrs.	29
Duval	7
Earl of Lichfield	61
Edison and Barnum's Electric Picture Company	92
Edwards, J.H.	27
Edwards, Norman	153
Elgar, Edward	85
Ellingham, Simon	64, 65
Elliot, George H.	51
Elmhurst, William	117
Elphinstone Jnr, James	140, 146, 147
Elphinstone Jnr, James (Bankruptcy)	147
Elphinstone Snr, James	35, 40, 43, 82, 147
Elphinstone, Charles G.W.	40, 43, 45, 93, 97, 102
Elphinstone, George	43, 97
Elphinstone's Circus, Hanley	82
Empire Theatre, Hanley	91
Empire Theatre, Longton	143
European Redevelopment Fund	109
Evans, Edith	51
Fair Lady Pit disaster	77
Fielding, Fenella	63
Fields, Gracie	103
Fisher, Colin	65

Fisher, Peter	117
Fontaine, Michael	64, 65
Ford, Richard	40
Forshaw, Edward	55
Fortescue, Mrs	150
Fuller, James	64
Gaiety Theatre of Varieties, Hanley	81
Gale, Fred	92
Garrett, Stephen	115
Gaston, V.M.	21
Gaumont Theatre, Hanley	105
Gaumont-British	107, 131
Gerry and the Pacemakers	107
Gingold, hermione	115
Gitana, Gertie	51
Glendinning, John	15
Godwin, Thomas	97, 125
Gold, Monica	21
Gordon Hotel, Stoke	125
Gordon Theatre and Opera House, Stoke	125
Goschen, W.	150
Graham, Elliot	35
Granada Television	117
Grand Theatre of Varieties, Hanley	97
Grant, James	93, 104
Grant, T.A.	45
Granville, Lord	77
Granville, Viscount	31
Great Row (Coal Seam)	109
Greaves, George	54, 55, 56
Green, ?	31
Green, Hughie	60
Greet, Ben	125
Greet, William	45
Greethead, James Frederick	81
Grice, Harry	153
Grogan, Martin	14
Grumbleweeds, The	67
Gummer, John	160
Hague, Samuel	77
Hales, Harold	27
Hall, Matthew	19
Hall, William	153
Halle Orchestra	85
Hamilton Baines, C.	21
Hanbridge Empire, The	102
Hanley and Shelton Philharmonic Society	77
Hanley Mission Society	78
Hanley Theatres	
Alexandra Music Hall	81
Batty's Circus	82
Central Hall	95
Central Lyric Hall	95
Century Theatre	112
Elphinstone's Circus	82
Empire	91
Gaiety Theatre of Varieties	81
Gaumont Theatre	105
Grand	97
Imperial Circus	76
Imperial Mission Hall	76
King's Palace	91

Lyric Hall	95
Mitchell Memorial Theatre	113
Myers' American Circus	70
New Inn	81
Odeon Theatre	105
People's Music Hall (II)	73
People's Varieties	77
Regent Theatre	105
Royal Alexandra Music Hall	81
Royal Pottery Theatre	31
Royal, The	31
Spitfire Mitchell Memorial Theatre	113
Theatre Royal	31
Theatre Royal, Grand Opera House and Temple of Varieties	70
Tontine Street Circus	82
Victoria Hall	85
Victoria Music Hall	70
Hanley Theatres and Circus	45, 92, 93, 97, 102
Hardy, Oliver	59
Hare, James	76
Harmston's Circus	82
Harrison, E.T.	76
Hartshill Theatres	
Victoria Theatre	115
Heathcote, Richard Edensor	7
Hengler, Charles	76
Hengler's Circus	76
Henry, E.B.	71
Hermann, Dr. Carl	99
Hill Samuel	62
Hill, Henry	143
Hinde, Thomas	38
Hinge, Doctor Evadne	63
Hippodrome, Burslem	19, 21
Hippodrome, Stoke	125
Holloway, James	71
Holloway, Stanley	51
Hoskins, Bob	118
Howe, W.	83
Hughes, Matthew	76
Hughes, Percy	51, 54, 59, 102
Huntbach, Alfred (Mayor of Hanley)	92
Hutchison, Emma	45
Hutchison, Percy	45
Hyde, R.M.	38
iM Properties	141, 160
Imperial Circus, Hanley	76
1882 Collapse	78
Imperial Mission Hall, Hanley	76
Inman, John	63
Inskips and Sons	149
Irving, H.B.	45
Irving, Sir Henry	148
Jackson and Sons, George	143
Jacobi, Sir Derek	111
Jacques, Hattie	52
James Davies Ltd	140
Jannings, Emil	107
Jolson, Al	107
Jomen's, Longton	141
Jones, W.	83
Jordan, Diane Louise	67

Old Theatres in the Potteries

Joseph, Lesley 111
Joseph, Michael 115
Joseph, Stephen 115, 117, 118, 119, 121
Jumpin' Jaks 69
Karno, Fred 102
Keane, Osborne 15
Keates (Printers) 52
Kelly, Woody 99
Kenealy, Dr. 12
Kennedy, B. 92
Kent, George Charles 143
Kenwright, Bill 62, 66
Key, Charles 55
Killjoys, The 62
Kinemacolor 161
King's Palace Theatre, Hanley 91
Kingsley, Ben 118
Kingston, Mabel 93
Kirkham, Mr. (Mayor of Stoke) 92
KPMG 69
Lane, Terry 119
Lathom, Countess of 102
Lathom, Lady 150
Laurel, Stan 59
Lea, Miss. Lillian 98
Leason, William T. (Lord Mayor) 107
Leeds and Hanley Theatres of Varieties
.... 92
Lester, Harry 59
Levitt Bernstein Associates 85, 109
Lind, Jenny 7
Lindsay, Robert 64
Liquid nightclub 69
Littler, Emile 56
Lloyd, Mike 66, 69
Lobley, Joseph 85
Logan, Arthur 56
Longton and District Theatre Company
.... 140, 143, 149
Longton Theatres ....
   Empire Theatre 143
   Panopticon Theatre 161
   Queen's Theatre 143
   Regent Theatre 163
   Royal Alma Theatre 137
   Royal Victoria 139
   Theatre Royal 139
Loretto, M. and Madam 70
Luminar Leisure 69
Lyceum Theatre, Burslem 14
Lynam, Beckett and Lynam 123
Lynne, Gillian 63
Lyric Hall, Hanley 95
Macnaghten, Frank 131
Madoc, Ruth 67
Magnus, Henry 7
Majestic Ballroom, Hanley 95
Manchester Palace of Varieties Limited
.... 102
Manning, Will 99
Martin, David 56
Matcham, Frank 40, 43, 91, 97, 148
Matthews, John 161
McDonald, Leslie 59

Meakin, George..................................85
Mecca Bingo Club at the Theatre Royal, Hanley 60
Melly, George.....................................73
Melville, Charles....................19, 42, 45
Messenger, Melinda...........................67
Mitchell Memorial Theatre, Hanley. 113
Mitchell, Reginald............................113
Mitcheson, Captain George A..........140
Molesworth, Ida..................................45
Monro, Matt......................................107
Moody Manners Opera......................45
Moore, J.P..92
Moorhouse, H.D...............................103
Morgan, Terence...............................131
Morton, William H...........................139
Moss Empires...........................59, 102
Mossfield Colliery disaster................147
Mountford, David Harding.....123, 125, 127
Mower, Patrick...................................63
Moxon, W.J..45
Mr. Smith's Nightclub, Hanley..........78
Municipal Hall, Newcastle...............115
Myers, J.W... 70
National Liberal Federation...............82
National Lottery, The.......................109
National Provincial Circuit Limited...45
Negro Minstrel Acts...........................75
New Inn, Hanley.................................81
New Roxy, Hanley, The......................78
Newcastle Amateur Operatic Society 107
Newcastle and Pottery Theatre............7
Newcastle-under-Lyme Theatres..........
   Municipal Hall............................115
   Planned Brampton Theatre.........115
   Theatre Royal..................................7
Newnham-Davis, Colonel................150
Newsome's Cirque..............................70
Nixon, Vyvian................................... 119
Norfolk, William...............................117
North Staffordshire Amateur Operatic and Dramatic Society........................23
North Staffordshire Regiment, Volunteer Batallion of.....................140
North Staffs. Amateur Operatic and Dramatic Society................................61
North Staffs. Amateur Operatic Society 51
O'Brien, Richard................................62
O'Connor M.P., Mr............................31
O'Connor, Des....................................67
Odeon Theatre, Hanley....................105
Orbison, Roy....................................107
Osbourne, Norman............................27
Owen and Ward (Architects)............125
Palmer, William J...............................77
Panopticon Theatre, Longton..........161
Patterson, Peter.................................117
Patti, Adelina......................................85
Pawson, Father John..........................63
Peake, Frederick..........................52, 54
Pearson, Major.................................. 82
Pedley, Charles.................................148
Pemberton, P...................................... 27

170

People's Hall, Hanley..........................31
People's Music Hall (II), Hanley........73
People's Varieties, Hanley....................77
Pestridge, James....................................56
Philips, W.D..146
Phipps, Charles J..................................40
Pickhull, Stephen...........................7, 32
Planned Brampton Theatre, Newcastle-under-Lyme...115
Porthill Players............................67, 111
Potteries Own, The...............................51
Potteries Theatres Ltd..........................45
Potteries Theatres Ltd..........................59
Powell, Annie......................................139
Powell, Peggy..56
Powell, Robert........................... 118, 121
Poynter, Chapman................................13
Poynter's New Theatre, Burslem.........13
Pridmore, Brian....................................65
Priest, Judas..85
Primitive Methodist Chapel, Brunswick Street, Hanley..31
Prince of Wales Theatre, Tunstall...........9
Prince, J...70
Provincial Cinematograph Theatres..105
Provincial Music Hall Company........91
Quayle, Anthony...................................63
Queen, Her Majesty The....................111
Queen's Theatre Production Society...25
Queen's Theatre, Burslem....................23
Queen's Theatre, Longton.................143
   1888 Opening............................ 146

1890 Elphinstone Jnr, James (Bankruptcy)...............................147
1890 Tearle, Edmund.................147
1894 Fire.......................................148
1894 Reconstruction..................148
1896 New Building....................149
1914 Empire Palace of Varieties..153
1922 Conversion to Cinema.......153
1952 Refurbishment...................156
1966 Civic Theatre..................... 157
1992 Fire.......................................160
Radiana...156
Rapley, Felton...........................105, 107
Ray, Milton... 92
Ray, Ted.. 51
Regent Theatre Trust........................108
Regent Theatre, Hanley....................105
   1929 Opening............................ 107
   1950 Gaumont............................107
   1974 Tripling...............................108
   1976 Odeon................................ 108
   1995 Rebuilding.........................109
   1999 Reopening..........................111
Regent Theatre, Longton..................163
Reiner, Carl.. 64
Repertory Players..............................135
Repertory Theatre, Stoke..........135, 157
Revill, Wallace....................................140
Revolution, Hanley...........................104
Richard, Cliff..................................... 107
Ridley, John..112
Rigby, James.......................................139

Ritz, G.J.	70
Roberts, Mr. and Mrs.	71
Roberts, T.	9
Robeson, Paul	85
Robinson, Tony	119
Roden, Colonel	73
Rodgers, Mrs. T.	40
Rogers, Clodagh	63
Rogers, James	32
Rogers, T.	40
Rogers, Thomas	33, 71, 73, 76
Rolling Stones, The	107
Rose, T.B.	32
Ross, Gertrude	21
Ross, R.	27
Ross, Raymond	119
Royal Alexandra Music Hall, Hanley	81
Royal Alma Theatre, Longton	137
Royal Britannia Theatre, Burslem	14
Royal Pottery Theatre, Hanley	31
Royal Victoria Theatre, Longton	139
Sadler's Wells Ballet	52, 54
Sadler's Wells Opera	52
Salmo, Juno	99
Salvation Army	12, 78, 82
Salvation Mission, The	15
Sambrook, John	121
Sargent, Malcolm	85
Savage, Warwick	21
Sea Lion Public House, Hanley	7
Second City Management	61
Seyler, Athene	51
Seymour, Tom	27
Shapiro, Helen	107
Shaw, T.E.	35
Shelley's Laserdome, Longton	161
Slater, Arthur	29
Sleep, Wayne	63
Smith B.E.M, W.	52
Smith, Miss. (The Gypsy Lass)	77
Smith, Rodney "Gypsy"	15, 77, 82
Smith, Ted	111
Snape, John (Senior)	7, 14
Snape, John William	14
Snape's Theatre, Burslem	14
Spencroft (Coal Seam)	109
Spicer, Gregory	139
Spitfire Mitchell Memorial Theatre, Hanley	113
Spode, Josiah	7
Springfield, Dusty	78
St. James' Theatre, Tunstall	9
St. Simon and St. Jude, Shelton	135
Stardust, Alvin	63
Steele, Laurence	135
Stephenson, Dennis	65
Steward, Don	65, 66
Stoddard, Hal	15
Stoke Theatres	
Crown Theatre	123
Gordon Theatre and Opera House	125
Hippodrome	125
Repertory Theatre	135

Stoke-on-Trent Amateur Operatic Society..................51, 59, 64
Stoke-on-Trent and North Staffordshire Theatre Trust..................119
Stoke-on-Trent Dramatic Society.....135
Stoney, Heather..................117, 121
Stratton, Eugene..................127
Strike, 1881 Pottery..................14
Stuart, Basil..................19
Studio Theatre Company.........115, 119
Suee Seen, Miss..................29
Sutherland, Duchess of..................150
Talbot, Richard..................108
Taprogge, Angela..................63
Taylor, Arthur..................9
Taylor, John (Architect)............143, 147
Tearle, Edmund..................147, 148
Temple of Thespis..................7
Temple of Varieties, Hanley..................70
Terry, Ellen..................45
Terson, Peter..................117, 119, 120
Theatre Royal, Hanley..................31
   1850 People's Hall..................31
   1852 Royal Pottery Theatre..........33
   1871 Theatre Royal and Opera House..................38
   1887 Theatre Royal..................40
   1894 Theatre Royal..................43
   1949 Fire..................52
   1951 Theatre Royal..................55
   1961 Closure..................59
   1982 Reopening..................61
   1993 Reopening..................64
   1994 Reopening..................65
   1997 The Royal..................66
   2000 Final Closure..................69
   Development of the Theatre Royal, Hanley..................34
Theatre Royal, Longton..................139
Theatre Royal, Newcastle-under-Lyme.7
Theatre Royal, Tunstall..................9
Thorne, Richard Samuel..................33
Thorne, William Shuker..................32
Till, P.C. 52
Todd, Richard..................156
Tontine Street Circus, Hanley............82
Top Hat Club, Hanley..................60
Townsend, Reverend G..................127
Trent, W.E. 105
Trevelyan, Lady..................120
Trinder, Tommy..................156
Tunstall Theatres..................
   Prince of Wales..................9
   St. James..................9
   Theatre Royal..................9
Turner, J. 42
Turner, John..................143
Turner, Tubby..................51
Victoria Hall, Hanley..................85
Victoria Music Hall, Hanley..................70
Victoria Theatre Club, Hartshill.......117
Victoria Theatre, Hartshill..................115
   1967 Controversy..................118
Wade, Sir George..................121
Wainratta, The Brothers..................71

Wall, Max 51	Wild, Jack 66
Wallace-Copland, H 56	Wilkes, Jonathan 25, 111
Walters, A.E. 143	Williams, G.E. 153
Walters, A.S. 148	Williams, Robbie 25
Wardhaugh, Matthew 7, 137, 139	Williamson, H. H. 7
Warrilow, J. 71, 73	Windley, John 70, 71
Waters, Hampton 143	Wolfit, Donald 56
Watts, Dodo 78	Wonder, Stevie 107
Webberley's, Hanley 135	Wood, Goldstraw and Yorath 113
Wedgwood Theatre, Burslem 19	Wood, John 7
Wedgwood, Josiah 7	Wurlitzer organ 105, 107
Westcott, Jessie 12	York, Peter 65
Wilcox, Toyah 63	

References

SOTCA refers to availability at the
Stoke-on-Trent City Archives

Old Theatres in the Potteries

Old Theatres in the Potteries

1 "The Royal Theatre at Newcastle", Staffordshire Sentinel Summer Number, June 1910, SOTCA

2 "The Theatre in the Potteries", Staffordshire Sentinel Summer Number, June 1906, SOTCA

3 "Sixty Years Recollections of an Etruscan", John Finney, SOTCA

4 "A History of the County of Stafford: Volume 8", edited by J.G. Jenkins

5 The Era, 16/03/1851

6 The Era, 29/09/1864

7 Staffordshire Advertiser, 07/10/1865

8 The Era, 16/07/1865

9 Reynold's Weekly Newspaper, 02/02/1866

10 The Era, 20/11/1873

11 "Old Times in the Potteries", William Scarratt, SOTCA

12 The Era, 17/03/1878

13 The Era, 21/09/1879

14 The Era, 23/04/1881

15 Liverpool Mercury, 10/10/1882

16 The Era, 25/05/1951

17 Manchester Guardian, 04/05/1850

18 Pall Mall Gazette, 21/03/1870

19 The Era, 17/09/1871

20 Birmingham Daily Post, 09/07/1872

21 The Era, 21/07/1872

22 The Era, 24/10/1891

23 The Era, 13/05/1877

24 The Era, 10/08/1880

25 Staffordshire Sentinel, 04/05/1881

26 Birmingham Daily Post, 01/12/1881

27 "Studies in the sources of Arnold Bennett's Novels", L. Tillier, SOTCA

28 The Era, 10/05/1882, The Era, 17/02/1883

29 The Era, 27/05/1882

30 Staffordshire Sentinel, 19/04/1884

31 "A History of the County of Stafford: Volume 8", edited by J.G. Jenkins, SOTCA

32 The Era, 17/09/1887

33 "What happened when the theatre came to town 100 years ago", Six Towns Magazine, Aug 1963

34 "Rendezvous with the Past", Staffordshire Sentinel Newspapers, 1954, SOTCA

35 The Era, 01/12/1888, 27/06/1891

36 Staffordshire Sentinel, 28/01/1896

37 *Your Own, Your Very Own*, in That's Entertainment. Adapted from BBC Radio Stoke series.

38 The Era, 11/04/1896

39 The Stage, 13/06/1907 (as Wedgwood Theatre), 17/10/1907 (as Hippodrome)

40 The Victoria County History could not find a date for this move back in 1963. The surviving Burslem Council minutes for the time make no reference to the move, however those for the year 1907 are missing, and by August 1909, the *Staffordshire Sentinel* reports the site of the new municipal buildings as being wasteland. As the postal address for both sites was the same, Wedgwood Place, advertisements and programmes are of no help. Until the local newspapers are digitised, I expect that the exact date will remain a mystery, although it is likely it occurred at the same time as the renaming to the *Hippodrome*. See 40.

41 "Amusements in the Potteries", SOTCA

42 The Stage, 04/05/1916

43 Evening Sentinel, 20/12/1947

44 The Sentinel, 26/01/2009

45 "Ninety Years of Cinema in the Potteries", Brian Hornsey

46 "Report Concerning possible use of Queen's Hall as a Civic Theatre", November 1966, SOTCA

47 Stoke-on-Trent City Council Minutes, General Purposes Committee, 10/01/1967, SOTCA

48 http://www.youtube.com/watch?v=sabTqbBcoCg, as of September 2010

49 http://www.queenstheatreburslem.com/History.htm, September 2010

50 The Theatres Trust Theatre Database

51 Evening Sentinel, 13/11/1914

52 Evening Sentinel, 17/11/1914

53 Evening Sentinel, 16/11/1917

54 Evening Sentinel, 10/12/1917

55 "Give my Regards to the Broadway", Barry Blaize, SOTCA

56 "The Borough of Stoke-upon-Trent", John Ward, 1843, SOTCA

57 "History of Methodism in the Potteries", T.A. Lloyd, SOTCA

58 Theatre Royal and Opera House – Declaration of Trusts 1873, SOTCA

59 White's History, Gazetteer and Directory of Staffordshire, 1851, SOTCA

60 Reynold's Weekly Newspaper, 05/05/1850

61 The Lever, 08/03/1851, SOTCA

62 The Lever, 15/05/1851, SOTCA

63 Staffordshire Advertiser, 24/01/1852

64 Staffordshire Advertiser, 04/09/1852

65 The Era, 12/09/1852

66 Staffordshire Advertiser, 20/11/1852, 27/11/1852, 04/12/1852

67 Staffordshire Advertiser, 12/12/1852

68 The Era, 10/04/1854

69 Staffordshire Advertiser, 27/12/1856

70 Staffordshire Advertiser, 23/06/1857

71 Marked difference in shape/size of building between 1857 Homer map and 1865 OS Map

72 Staffordshire Advertiser, 11/07/1857

73 Staffordshire Advertiser, 11/07/1857

74 Staffordshire Advertiser, 08/08/1857

75 Birmingham Daily Post, 30/09/1859

76 "The Theatre in the Potteries", Staffordshire Sentinel Summer Number, June 1906, SOTCA

77 Liverpool Mercury, 17/11/1865

78 "The Ancient Corporation of Hanley", W.D. Spranton, 1901

79 Staffordshire Sentinel, 04/03/1871

80 The Era, 12/03/1871

81 "Footlights", Edition 1 notes remains of gallery supports to west of site, SOTCA

82 The Era, 21/04/1872

83 The Era, 17/02/1856, The Stage, 09/06/1949

84 Theatre Programme Collection at SOTCA

85 Birmingham Daily Post, 22/01/1884

86 Potteries, Newcastle and District 1907 Reference Directory, SOTCA

87 Staffordshire Sentinel, 01/08/1887

88 Staffordshire Sentinel, 02/08/1887

89 Staffordshire Advertiser, 06/08/1887

90 Staffordshire Sentinel, 03/08/1894

91 The Era, 18/04/1888

92 "The Theatre in the Potteries", Staffordshire Sentinel Summer Number, June 1906, SOTCA

93 The Era, 04/08/1894

94 Staffordshire Sentinel, 03/08/1894

95 Staffordshire Sentinel, 07/08/1894

96 Potteries, Newcastle and District 1907 Reference Directory, SOTCA

97 Theatre Programme Collection at SOTCA

98 The London Gazette, 09/10/1900

99 The Stage, 12/08/1909

100 Manchester Guardian, 16/02/1931

101 The Stage, 14/10/1920

102 Evening Sentinel, 02/06/1949

103 The Stage, 01/09/1921

104 Ninety Years of Cinema in the Potteries, Brian Hornsey, SOTCA

105 Evening Sentinel, 14/09/1934

106 "Recollections of a Theatre Manager", Thats Entertainment!, SOTCA

107 Evening Sentinel, 04/11/1939

108 Evening Sentinel, 12/03/1940

109 Evening Sentinel, 20/02/1940

110 Evening Sentinel, 14/04/1940

111 Theatre Programme Collection, SOTCA

112 "Recollections of a Theatre Manager", Thats Entertainment!, SOTCA

113 Evening Sentinel, 02/06/1949

114 "The Fire of '49", Footlights No. 2, SOTCA

115 Evening Sentinel, 02/06/1949

116 "A Phoenix out of the Ashes", Footlights No.3, SOTCA

117 The Times, 02/06/1949, 06/06/1949

118 "The Fire of '49", Footlights No. 2, SOTCA

119 Evening Sentinel, 02/06/1949

120 The Stage, 09/06/1949

121 Evening Sentinel, 04/06/1949

122 Evening Sentinel, 16/09/1949

123 Evening Sentinel, 11/04/1950

124 Footlights 2, SOTCA

125 Evening Sentinel, 1950 (Undated)

126 Evening Sentinel, 01/05/1951

127 Images on Flickr, http://www.flickr.com/photos/stagedoor/2670352217/

128 Programme for "Annie Get Your Gun", 14/08/1951, SOTCA

129 "Jottings from a Notebook", John Abberley, SOTCA

130 Evening Sentinel 01/05/1951

131 Evening Sentinel 14/08/1951

132 Footlights 3, SOTCA

133 Evening Sentinel, 15/08/1951

134 Programme for "Annie Get Your Gun", 14/08/1951, SOTCA

135 The Way We Were, March 2002, SOTCA

136 "Recollections of a Theatre Manager", Thats Entertainment, SOTCA

137 The Times, 21/06/1958

138 "Recollections of a Theatre Manager", Thats Entertainment, SOTCA

139 The Stage, 27/07/1961

140 Evening Sentinel, 08/07/1961

141 Weekly Sentinel, 21/10/1961

142 The Times (not The Times of London), 25/10/1966

143 Stoke-on-Trent City Council Minutes, Cultural Activities Sub-committee, 13/12/1966

144 "On Stage with J.S.A" from Evening Sentinel, from the week of 28/11/1966
145 Evening Sentinel, 10/09/1981
146 Evening Sentinel, 22/09/1981
147 Footlights No. 3, SOTCA
148 Evening Sentinel, 06/01/1982
149 Evening Sentinel, 01/09/1982
150 Evening Sentinel, 23/07/1982
151 Evening Sentinel, 16/11/1982
152 Evening Sentinel, 16/12/1982
153 Evening Sentinel, 14/12/1982
154 Evening Sentinel, 31/12/1982
155 Evening Sentinel, 18/01/1983
156 Evening Sentinel, 29/01/1983
157 Evening Sentinel, 18/01/1982
158 Evening Sentinel, 10/03/1983
159 Evening Sentinel, 28/03/1983
160 Evening Sentinel, 22/08/1988
161 Evening Sentinel, 03/09/1985
162 Evening Sentinel, 14/08/1987
163 Evening Sentinel, 22/07/1988
164 "The Stage is Set for a Great Future", Theatre Royal Plc., 1984. SOTCA
165 Evening Sentinel, 07/05/1984
166 Rocky Horror Show – Final Week Souvenir Programme, 1988. SOTCA
167 Evening Sentinel, 22/07/1988
168 Evening Sentinel, 21/8/1984
169 *The Personality Test*, broadcast on BBC Radio 4, 02/08/2007
170 Evening Sentinel, 14/06/1988
171 The Stage, 28/06/1987
172 Evening Sentinel, 26/06/1987, 29/06/1987
173 Evening Sentinel, 25/11/1987
174 Evening Sentinel, 27/04/1990
175 Evening Sentinel, 11/03/1993
176 Evening Sentinel, 06/03/1993
177 Evening Sentinel, 04/03/1993
178 Evening Sentinel, 18/06/1993
179 The Times 01/011997, Birmingham Post 03/12/1998, Evening Sentinel 02/07/1999, Independent on Sunday 20/04/2003, The Guardian 04/10/1995, 26/01/1996

180 Evening Sentinel, 03/08/1993
181 Evening Sentinel, 04/08/1993
182 Evening Sentinel, 25/09/1993
183 Evening Sentinel, 18/09/1993
184 Evening Sentinel, 27/10/1993
185 Evening Sentinel, 10/12/1993
186 Evening Sentinel, 21/05/1994
187 Evening Sentinel, 03/02/1994
188 Evening Sentinel, 14/07/1994
189 Evening Sentinel, 25/06/1994
190 Evening Sentinel, 22/07/1994
191 Evening Sentinel, 17/04/1994
192 The Stage, 20/02/1997
193 The Stage, 29/06/2005
194 Evening Sentinel, 14/04/1995
195 Evening Sentinel, 01/09/1994
196 The Stage, 03/11/1994
197 Evening Sentinel, 14/04/1995
198 The Sentinel, 09/03/1996
199 The Sentinel, 24/04/1996
200 The Stage, 23/05/1996
201 The Sentinel, 09/08/1996
202 The Guardian, 03/09/2006
203 The Sentinel, 24/10/1996
204 The Sentinel, 02/11/1996
205 The Sentinel, 19/09/1997
206 "The Silent Stage", Alan J. Barnett, SOTCA
207 The Sentinel, 11/12/1997
208 The Sentinel, 13/07/2000
209 The Stage, 08/06/2000
210 Staffordshire Advertiser, 16/06/1864
211 The Era, 12/06/1864
212 Staffordshire Advertiser, 27/08/1864
213 Liverpool Mercury, 21 9 64
214 The Era, 27/08/1865
215 The Era, 06/04/1866
216 The Era, 14/06/1867

217 Birmingham Daily Post, 21/01/1868

218 The Era, 14/08/1870

219 The Era, 04/12/1870

220 The Era, 25/12/1870

221 The Era, 18/09/1871

222 The Era, 30/02/1879

223 Birmingham Daily Post, 25/10/1871

224 The Era, 29/06/1873, 17/08/1873, 21/09/1873, 20/10/1878

225 Staffordshire Sentinel, week of 21/07/1873

226 Weekly Sentinel, 19/07/1873, Daily Sentinel 21/07/1873, Staffordshire Advertiser, 26/07/1873

227 Weekly Sentinel, 16/08/1873

228 The Era, 17/08/1879

229 Birmingham Daily Post, 03/03/1877

230 The Era, 21/01/1878

231 The Era, 03/03/1878

232 Staffordshire Sentinel, 17/09/1878, 21/09/1878

233 Staffordshire Sentinel, 14/09/1878

234 Imperial Circus Plan, made by the Borough Surveyor. SOTCA. CS/D/92

235 Staffordshire Sentinel, 16/09/1878, 18/09/1878, 21/09/1878, Staffordshire Advertiser 21/09/1878

236 The Era, 30/02/1879

237 Birmingham Daily Post, 24/11/1880

238 The Times, 08/11/1887

239 Birmingham Daily Post, 02/02/1880

240 Birmingham Daily Post, 17/05/1883

241 Staffordshire Sentinel, 18/03/1881, The Era 26/03/1881

242 The Era, 19/03/1881

243 Lloyd's Weekly Newspaper, 29/10/1882

244 Manchester Guardian, 23/10/1882, The Illustrated Police News, 04/11/1882

245 Staffordshire Sentinel, 15/02/1897

246 "A History of the County of Stafford: Volume 8", edited by J.G. Jenkins

247 Staffordshire Sentinel, 03/11/1908

248 Stoke-on-Trent Council Minutes, 1912

249 Ninety Years of Cinema in the Potteries, Brian Hornsey

250 "The Way We Were", Staffordshire Sentinel News & Media, August 2010

251 Ordnance Survey, 1:500 Town Plan, 1st Edition

252 The Theatres Trust Database

253 Staffordshire Sentinel, 23/12/1884

254 The Era, 1887

255 Rendezvous with the Past, Staffordshire Sentinel Newspapers, 1954

256 The Era, 10/10/1880

257 The Era, 10/04/1886

258 Northern Territory Times and Gazette, 25/11/1882

259 The Times, 17/02/1885

260 The Era, 08/10/1884

261 The Era, 12/03/1887

262 The Era, 10/01/1881, 25/08/1888

263 Ticket at SOTCA

264 "The Grand Tour", Neville Malkin

265 "Music in the Five Towns", Reginald Nettle

266 Programme Collection at SOTCA

267 Levitt Bernstein Website

268 Theatre Programme Collection at SOTCA

269 The Era, 20/02/1892

270 Manchester Guardian, 09/02/1892

271 Staffordshire Sentinel, 15/03/1892

272 "Give my Regards to the Broadway", Barry Blaize

273 The Era, 21/12/1899, Manchester Guardian 20/12/1899, The Times 20/12/1899

274 The Stage, 30/07/1903

275 The Era, 01/04/1899

276 Staffordshire Sentinel, 09/04/1901

277 "Your Own, Your Very Own" in That's Entertainment, adapted from BBC Radio Stoke

278 Ninety Years of Cinema in the Potteries, Brian Hornsey

279 Amusements in the Potteries, SOTCA

280 Manchester Guardian, 24/05/1924

281 "The Lost Empire", Barry Blaize, Images contained therein.

282 Kelly's Directory of Staffordshire, 1896

283 Potteries, Newcastle and District Directory, 1912

284 "The Lost Empire", Barry Blaize

285 "The Way We Were", Staffordshire Sentinel News and Media, August 2010

286 The Era 10/04/1897

287 Staffordshire Sentinel, 10/08/1898

288 Staffordshire Sentinel, 23/08/1898

289 Victoria and Albert Museum Online Collections

290 Staffordshire Sentinel, 01/12/1908

291 "Chaplin Stage by Stage", A.J. Marriott

292 "Studies in the sources of Arnold Bennett's Novels", Tillier

293 Staffordshire Sentinel, 06/12/1909

294 'The Hanbridge Empire', "Paris Nights: And Other Impressions of Places and People", A. Bennett

295 Theatre Programme Collection at SOTCA

296 Grand Historical Article, from Staffordshire Sentinel, Local Newscuttings at SOTCA

297 The Stage, 14/10/1920

298 "Grand Theatre, Hanley; Alterations; Plans, sections and elevations", DT.TRM/1/107-129, Tyne and Wear Archive Service

299 Evening Sentinel, 11/05/1932, "Recollections of a Theatre Manager" in That's Entertainment

300 "The Lost Empire", Barry Blaize

301 Manchester Guardian, 23/03/1932

302 Evening Sentinel, 11/05/1932

303 Evening Sentinel 23/11/1934

304 The Theatres Trust Database

305 "The Regent Story", Richard Talbot

306 Staffordshire Sentinel, 07/02/1929

307 www.ukwurlitzer.co.cc

308 English Heritage at www.heritagegateway.org.uk

309 Evening Sentinel, 21/03/1994

310 Evening Sentinel, 03/09/1994

311 Evening Sentinel 07/05/1994

312 "A West End for Stoke-on-Trent", Chief Executive's Department, SOTCA

313 The Sentinel, 24/05/1996, 25/11/1996

314 The Sentinel, 22/09/1999

315 http://www.jamesandtaylor.co.uk/m1/m1_s14_3.htm

316 Regent Theatre Technical Specification, SOTCA

317 The Stage, 27/09/2001, http://www.building.co.uk/news/levitt-bernstein-wins-%C2%A3125m-from-stoke-council/1011670.article, as of September 2010

318 The Sentinel, 23/09/1999

319 The Sentinel, 02/08/2010

320 "Century Theatre in Staffordshire", Staffordshire Life, Summer No. 1956

321 Debrett's People of Today

322 Evening Sentinel 13/05/1960, 10/06/1960, 17/06/1960

323 Evening Sentinel, 01/03/1943

324 Evening Sentinel Special Supplement, 28/10/1957

325 http://www.sgfl.org.uk/mitchell_theatre/theatre, as of September 2010

326 BBC Stoke News Article, Mitchell Memorial Theatre renovation is 'on schedule' 09/03/2010

327 "Actor and Architect", Introduction by Stephen Joseph

328 "The Repertory Movement", G. Rowell & A. Jackson

329 "Theatre in the Round", Stephen Joseph

330 Evening Sentinel, 27/07/1960

331 Cheadle and Tean Times, 19/05/1961

332 Evening Sentinel, 31/10/1963

333 Theatre Programme Collection at SOTCA

334 The Sentinel, 31/10/2008

335 Express and Star, 04/02/1969

336 The Guardian, 19/01/1967

337 The Times, 11/01/1967

338 The Times, 23/01/1967

339 Evening Sentinel, 23/02/1967

340 Evening Sentinel, 28/04/1967

341 The Times, 13/03/1967

342 Evening Sentinel, 31/03/1967, 04/04/1967

343 Theatre Programme Collection at SOTCA

344 Evening Sentinel, 30/04/1967

345 Stoke-on-Trent City Council Minutes, Cultural Activities Sub-committee, 1967

346 The Guardian, 07/06/1967

347 Evening Sentinel, 11/07/1967

348 The Guardian, 04/09/1967

349 The Guardian, 01/05/1967

350 Evening Sentinel, 15/09/1970

351 Evening Sentinel, 08/12/1977

352 Evening Sentinel, 14/02/1978

353 Evening Sentinel, 01/03/1978

354 Evening Sentinel, 02/10/1980

355 Evening Sentinel, 28/4/1983

356 New Victoria Theatre, Opening Programme, at SOTCA

357 Evening Sentinel, 12/05/1984

358 Evening Sentinel, 11/03/1985

359 The Era, 20/02/1897

360 Staffordshire Sentinel, 13/02/1897

361 Fenns Borough Almanack 1900

362 Staffordshire Sentinel, 16/02/1897

363 The Era, 20/02/1897

364 The Stage, 09/02/1899

365 Manchester Guardian, 07/02/1899

366 Staffordshire Advertiser, 17/03/1900, The Stage, 13/03/1900

367 Staffordshire Sentinel, 13/03/1900

368 Manchester Guardian, 02/04/1901

369 "Your Own, Your Very Own", from That's Entertainment, adapted from BBC Radio Stoke

370 Staffordshire Sentinel, 01/11/1904

371 Theatre Programme Collection at SOTCA

372 Evening Sentinel, 25/07/1952

373 Ninety Years of Cinema in the Potteries, Brian Hornsey

374 "Stoke-on-Film The Seventies", Ray Johnson

375 "Golden Jubilee Souvenir Programme 1920-1970", SOTCA, Manchester Guardian 28/03/1933

376 Ordnance Survey Town Plan, 1:500, 1850s

377 Longton's Shakespearean Mayor, Charles Lovatt

378 "Rendezvous with the Past", Staffordshire Sentinel Newspapers, 1954

379 Birmingham Daily Post, 31/01/1860

380 Ordnance Survey, 'County' Series, XVIII.10, 1878

381 Staffordshire Sentinel, 11/01/1868

382 The Theatres Trust Database

383 Staffordshire Advertiser, 18/01/1868

384 "Longton's Shakespearean Mayor", Charles Lovatt

385 Staffordshire Sentinel, 10/11/1883

386 "A History of Longton" J.H.Y. Briggs

387 The Era, 10/03/1888

388 Birmingham Daily Post, 29/05/1888

389 The Era, 22/12/1888

390 Birmingham Daily Post, 13/11/1888

391 Staffordshire Sentinel, 01/01/1889

392 Birmingham Daily Post, 08/03/1890

393 Keates' Gazetteer, 1892

394 Staffordshire Sentinel, 12/06/1895

395 Kelly's Directory of Staffordshire, 1904, Potteries, Newcastle and District Directory, 1907

396 Evening Sentinel, 06/05/1949, "Longton's Shakespearean Mayor", Charles Lovatt

397 Stoke-on-Trent Telephone Directory, 1987

398 Staffordshire Sentinel, 11/09/1888

399 The Era, 21/10/1888

400 Staffordshire Sentinel, 11/09/1888

401 Staffordshire Sentinel, 08/09/1888

402 The Stage, 14/09/1888

403 Staffordshire Sentinel, 29/12/1888

404 Staffordshire Sentinel, 30/09/1889

405 Staffordshire Sentinel, 28/10/1889

406 Staffordshire Advertiser, 15/03/1890

407 Staffordshire Advertiser, 04/09/1890, 29/09/1894

408 Staffordshire Sentinel, 16/09/1890

409 The Era, 04/03/1893

410 Birmingham Daily Post, 06/04/1893

411 The Era, 06/10/1894, Staffordshire Advertiser, 29/09/1894, Staffordshire Sentinel 28/09/1894, The Stage, 04/10/1894

412 Birmingham Daily Post, 02/10/1894

413 The Era, 15/12/1894

414 Staffordshire Sentinel, 22/06/1895, The Era, 15/06/1895

415 Staffordshire Sentinel, 15/05/1896

416 The Era, 08/02/1896

417 Potteries, Newcastle and District Directory, 1912, Staffordshire Sentinel, 15/05/1895

418 This was deemed a very important feature due to the Victoria Hall, Sunderland accident of 1883, where 184 children died of compressive asphyxia when a large group of children stampeded towards a blocked exit door.

419 The Stage, 14/05/1896

420 "City of Stoke-on-Trent Civic Theatre. Report of City Architect, Planning and Reconstruction Officer to Cultural Activities Sub-committee. November 1966.", SOTCA

421 The Era, 13/05/1896

422 Staffordshire Sentinel, 19/06/1896

423 Staffordshire Sentinel, 09/11/1904

424 Theatre Programme Collection at SOTCA

425 Staffordshire Sentinel, 26/04/1904

426 Staffordshire Sentinel, 04/08/1914

427 Manchester Guardian, 22/11/1921

428 Staffordshire Sentinel, 31/12/1921, 21/01/1922, 24/01/1922

429 Theatre Programme Collection at SOTCA

430 "The Grand Tour", Neville Malkin

431 "Our Haunted Kingdom", Andrew Green

432 Evening Sentinel, 26/07/1952

433 "City of Stoke-on-Trent Civic Theatre. Report of City Architect, Planning and Reconstruction Officer to Cultural Activities Sub-committee. November 1966.", SOTCA; Stoke-on-Trent City Council Minutes, Cultural Activities Sub-committee, 1966, SOTCA

434 English Heritage, via www.heritagegateway.org.uk

435 Curtains!!! or, A New Life for Old Theatres, 1982

436 Evening Sentinel, 23/06/1992

437 The Stage, 14/01/1993

438 Evening Sentinel, 01/01/1993

439 Evening Sentinel, 31/03/1995

440 The Sentinel, 11/01/1997

441 English Heritage, via www.heritagegateway.org.uk

442 Ninety Years of Cinema in the Potteries, Brian Hornsey

443 Amusements in the Potteries, SOTCA

444 Stoke-on-Trent Council Minutes, 1912

445 "Normacot and Longton filmed from January - June 1994", Mark Watson, DVD, SOTCA

446 Ninety Years of Cinema in the Potteries, Brian Hornsey

447 Amusements in the Potteries, SOTCA

448 The Stage, 01/09/1921

Lightning Source UK Ltd.
Milton Keynes UK
UKOW042132130812

197491UK00005B/92/P